The Spirit Within

liberty forrest

The Spirit Within

Copyright © 2012 liberty forrest

ALL RIGHTS RESERVED. Any unauthorised reprint or use of this material is prohibited. No part of this book may be reproduced or transmitted in any form or by any means, electronic or mechanical, including photocopying, recording, or by any information storage and retrieval system without express written permission from the author.

ISBN: 1481214578

ISBN-13: 978-1481214575

The Spirit Within

"Outstanding! There are really no words to adequately describe what liberty has written in this collection of short stories. Only someone who has come back from a higher plane could know as much as she does. liberty uses a very unique style of story-telling to convey many experiences to which all of us can relate.

"I believe liberty forrest is one of the literary geniuses of our time. I have never read anything as wonderful in my life. The stories in this book are stylistically different, and spellbinding.

"This is no ordinary woman; she has been to the spirit world before, and has revisited us to learn more lessons in life and to teach us what she has learned. She is a truly remarkable woman and writer.

"An entertainingly, brilliant read."

-- Pat Senior, Cheshire, England

"I found this book to be fantastic. I have read lots of healing books but never one that really shifted me into looking at my life in a totally different way, especially after reading the title story.

"After I finished reading 'The Spirit Within,' I now look at my life in a different light, a positive light. It has changed my perspective on my life. Now I see that there is a light at the end of the tunnel and I WILL make it."

-- Diane Smith, Alberta

The Spirit Within

Table of Contents

GHOSTLY ECHOS 1
GRIEF 4
THE GREEDY ARTIST'S AWAKENING 6
LETHAL MEMORIES 54
I AM DEVOURED 56
THE STORY OF TRUST 58
HOPE 71
THE SPIRIT WITHIN 80
ABOUT THE AUTHOR 131
CONNECT WITH THE AUTHOR 132
OTHER BOOKS BY LIBERTY FORREST 132

The Spirit Within

GHOSTLY ECHOS

I remember so vividly the land around The Farm and the intense feelings I had about it. As we drew nearer, I would become so excited it always felt as though the car was barely moving, like when you're trying to run in a dream and you feel like your legs are in quicksand, and it was all I could do not to get out and push the stupid car.

At the top of the last hill was the old one-room schoolhouse and lots of trees and shrubbery hiding the intersecting roads; hence, the long-practiced custom of honking just before you got there. Just a short distance away, there was one last curve -- oh, how I used to love that curve -- with its thick, lush, green trees and bushes lining the old dirt road, deep with familiar, somehow comforting ruts.

Finally, after we rounded the curve, there it was. The most delightful, wonderful, magical place on the face of the earth -- The Farm -- complete with a big, red barn, nestled into the trees around the curve. And of course there were other Farm delights, livestock, crabapple trees, fresh berries, the lake nearby, endless hours of laughter and exciting things to do, and most important of all, The House.

I wonder how much of my life has been spent in that house, although most of it was while I was 600 miles away. It was such a cosy old house, with its lovely creaking floors; soft, lumpy furniture, the Big Stool in the kitchen, which was SO tall and very difficult to climb; the pitcher and basin on the rough, wooden washstand in my room; the robin's-egg-blue walls throughout the entire house, and the doilies on everything; the old black wood stove; the familiar, rhythmic creaking and groaning of the green water pump in the utility room; the pail full of fresh, icy well water with a dipper in it, in case we were thirsty, and chamber pots for later; the ancient iron bed that swallowed me in its softness, feather pillows and quilts, sewn by my grandmother with love; heavenly smells of bread or cinnamon buns baking, chicken and dumplings, fresh, warm applesauce, and a myriad of other delights always filled the house -- I can still remember.

And I can still see Grandma standing in the kitchen, usually cooking. No one ever really loved me except Grandma. The House always warmed me when nothing else could ease the chill of my loneliness; even when I was far away, The Farm worked its magic. For years, the pain in my life was soothed only by the comforting memories, or anticipation of time spent on The Farm.

But now the roads are gravel; the ruts are gone. The desire to travel on them is gone. The trees and shrubs on the hill are gone; no one honks any more. A straight, bare, dry road now pushes its way through the place where the curve used to be. The barn is gone; burned to the ground. My grandmother and grandfather are gone. The meaning -- the all-important, soul-saving meaning is gone.

The House, however, is still there. The floors would creak more lovingly now, but no one walks on them any more, except the mice that scamper across them, in a hurry to hide from -- no one. The pitcher and basin are still there, but no one uses them any more. The furniture is softer and lumpier, but no one sits on it any more. The Big Stool isn't very big any more; in fact, it's small enough to be uncomfortable now. The heavenly warm kitchen smells have been replaced by dust, stale air, pungent mothballs (protecting what?). Grandma's sunny bedroom, which always smelled of her perfume, is gone, ripped apart after she died, and it was turned into a bathroom, now full of rusted fixtures from the lousy water.

If you stood ever so quietly and listened ever so carefully, you might still hear the lovely, soothing, rhythmic creaking and groaning of that old green water pump, as it filled buckets with water to be heated and dumped into a washtub for a child's late night bath in a darkened kitchen, lit only by the flickering fire in the stove.

If you closed your eyes and listened a little harder, you could hear the years' worth of sounds. They live in the walls. You could hear plates being scraped with silverware, as families delighted in the meals prepared with love; wooden matches being struck, followed by their tiny explosions; hushed voices, being careful not to wake the children (which generation? I can't make out the voices -- maybe the fourth?); the quiet scraping of potatoes as they are peeled, and the tiny splash as they are plunked into a pot of water; the snap of green beans before landing in a bowl; the crunch of crisp, fresh lettuce being torn; sick babies being nursed; squealing children; pages ripped off calendars, and voices remarking how quickly time is passing; crying -- who is that? There's so much pain -- can you hear it? Is it an echo of the sadness of someone who lived long ago, or is it the sobbing of a lonely ghost? Maybe it is I. When I close my eyes, I feel it.

So I don't close my eyes. I don't want to feel it. I don't want to remember. Besides, it's really not so different from the past. It's pretty much the same as before, isn't it? After all, it's just an empty farm, at the end of a gravel road, and just a rickety, old white house, always was, still is, but now occupied by birds and mice. It's just four sagging, old walls...walls that tell stories if you stand in the middle of them, close your eyes, and listen.

GRIEF

As we walk along a road by night, there is a certain and undeniable beauty that comes with the dark. Quaint aging houses, well-tended gardens and hedgerows, ancient stone paths, grand oak trees which seem like wise old sages, all are appreciated as in the day, but each displays a different character by moonlight.

And so it is when we witness the various stages experienced by a loved one as he or she draws nearer to the final major event in life, an event as powerful and intimate as birth. We still see the character and beauty of the soul that inhabited the body, and gave us the precious gift and joy of loving relationship, while at the same time, we begin to see the flame of life flickering and fading, and both soul and body become beings we no longer know well.

To witness the process of the death of a loved one is to be violated by Grief. It descends upon us unwanted, unbidden, yet we are powerless to prevent its firm grasp on our souls. It is rather like walking a lonely, dark road on a clear, still night and finding ourselves in the midst of a dense fog. It does not always happen in an instant, just one moment in time; indeed, sometimes it creeps in slowly, giving only the most vague suggestions that it is lurking just ahead.

We walk that deserted, lonely road, dark and cold, so still and quiet, as the mist gently drifts from place to place, seeming innocuous enough as it plays hide and seek, yet it is unmistakably eerie, its intentions not at all harmless or playful. At first, it hangs in patches, giving us small tastes of it, allowing us to carry on, walking through it. Occasionally, it dances away from the face of the moon, and once again, the road is illuminated by a loving memory of the one we've lost.

But as it gathers itself, as the mist begins to hang thick with what seem to be ghosts, appearing, then vanishing, changing shape and form, suddenly we are in its grasp, seemingly out of nowhere. We lose our sense of direction and our hearts begin to fill with fear, panic at the thought that we won't find our way out of it. What was once a bright, full moon, casting its soft glow upon the land, lighting the way of the traveller as it gives new light and life to all it sees, becomes, instead, a dim spectre, shrouded in billowing mist. Where once, we could witness its quiet radiance illuminating cobblestone roads, sleeping blossoms, and whispering leaves, gradually, the mist engulfs them, keeping them secret in its ethereal quality.

Then we, too, become surrounded and consumed by it, as it keeps us feeling alone, cut off from all life, existing in a terrible, and terrifying place. We feel frozen in fear, immobilized and unable to move, unable to find our way out, unable to see that the quaint, aging houses, the well-tended gardens, the grand oak trees, the sleeping blossoms and the whispering leaves are still there, and know that they are just hidden in Grief. It is as though they are gone from us forever, like the one we loved and lost, never to be seen or touched again. It is as though we, too, are gone, having been swallowed by it, becoming the ghosts that seem to live in the heavy mist that is Grief, appearing and vanishing, not quite of the Earth, unable to feel, to live -- becoming its undead.

THE GREEDY ARTIST'S AWAKENING

Once upon a time, there was a little boy who loved to paint. It made him as happy as the paintings were terrible. He thought he was brilliant and talented, and no one dared break his heart with the truth.

The boy missed the way his life had been when he was very young. But his father had been ill for some time, and could not manage much by way of work. The mother took in laundry, and tried to get some work cleaning homes, but there was not much work to be had. The family had been forced to move to a cramped little house where the three barely had room to turn around.

And so they struggled along, doing their best to make ends meet. There was very little food much of the time, and even less variety. Many times, a meal was a small portion of rice or a potato, but somehow, they carried on. Sometimes, there were vegetables from his mother's garden, when they had been able to obtain seeds and plant them. But then, much depended upon the weather conditions, and the seeds did not always yield much for all the effort that had gone into the garden.

And meat - oh, my goodness. What a treat, when his parents could scrape together a few coins to buy just a little, or when kind neighbours shared theirs. It broke his parents' hearts that they could not provide more for their son, but they loved him more than anything, and did the very best they could for him, happy to make whatever sacrifices they could.

But with each passing week, the boy became increasingly bitter and resentful about having such poor providers as parents. He detested their weakness. And he detested poverty. He swore that someday, he would become a rich and famous artist. He hated not having enough food. He despised having to worry that the family's home would be taken from them. He wanted to be able to buy absolutely anything and everything his heart desired, and still have enough money left over to do it a million times more. But how would he ever get to be a rich and famous artist, if he could not afford the supplies to practice painting?

Frustration simmered through the boy, sometimes reaching a boiling anger. Occasionally, a kind neighbour would bring him a few bits of paint or canvas. When he was old enough to begin doing odd jobs for villagers, he bought some art supplies every chance he got. It never occurred to him to offer any of his money to his parents to help them buy food or pay for other necessities; he thought only about his painting. His parents never asked him to contribute any of his earnings so that they could buy more food. Rather, they continued to do their best with what they had, and encouraged him to pursue his dream.

One spring day, it was announced at school that there would be an art contest, with a huge blue ribbon and a wide assortment of painting supplies as the prize. Of course, the boy was certain he would win, bringing him one step closer to his dream of being rich and famous.

Excitedly, he laboured over his painting for days, painstakingly creating what he believed was the winning masterpiece. And when he had finished, he stood back from his easel, admiring his work. Closing his eyes, he could just imagine the crowds cheering, and the judges saying that there had been no point in anyone else having entered because he was so obviously the winner.

Such daydreams gave the boy a bit of relief from his lonely life of poverty. They sustained him and gave him a goal, upon which he focused constantly. He obsessed about it, and how he detested the pitying expressions on the villagers' faces that left him feeling completely inadequate. Eagerly, he waited for the day when he would see looks of envy, as they admired his fame and his wealth.

From the day that the contest was announced, the boy could not wait to bring home the big blue ribbon. He would show his parents what it was to be successful; he would rise above this excuse for a life they had given him and teach them a thing or two about earning money.

Finally, the big day arrived. The boy carried his painting ever so carefully, all the way from home. With his chest puffed with pride, he anticipated the moment when the cloth would be removed, and there would be gasps of astonishment as all in attendance gazed upon his impressive work.

All the contestants were gathered together in the gymnasium, and each student stood beside an easel, upon which his or her painting rested, covered. When everyone was ready, the judges, teachers and parents were called in for the unveiling. The boy was fairly bursting with excitement when finally, the contestants were told to uncover their work.

As paintings were exposed, there were oohs and aaahs from the crowd, along with quiet whispers and low voices describing the beauty they beheld. Of course, the boy was confident that everyone was speaking about his masterpiece, and he stood, chest thrust forward, beaming.

It took some time for the judges to wander amongst the contestants, staring intently at each work of art, making notes, going back to some of them a few times. On occasion, the judges peered very closely at a painting, eyes squinting.

The boy decided that they must be trying to make the other contestants feel like they were really getting a fair chance at winning, since they had already decided who would come away with the blue ribbon, and would not want to offend the other children. Putting on his best 'humble' expression, he waited patiently for the moment that they announced him as the winner

It was some time before the judges finished their examinations of all work that had been entered in the contest. Then they spent more time whispering amongst themselves, looking at their notes, pointing at the paintings. 'Working out second and third place,' he thought to himself with a satisfied smile.

Finally, one of the judges stepped forward, and stood at a microphone in the center of the crowd. Clearing his throat, he began a short but moving speech about the talent and the effort that had been put forth by the contestants. Of course, he made the usual sort of statements to do with achieving goals, and with being proud of one's accomplishments. He said that although they could not all win the contest, each was a winner in his or her own way. Choosing a winner had been such a difficult choice, he said. The boy knew that the judge was just being polite, but he appreciated that it would be nice for those who did not win to hear such kind words.

A smug smile hung on the boy's face as the judge went on to announce the child who had taken third place. The crowd clapped and whistled as the happy child went up to receive his ribbon, the applause subsiding as he walked back to his painting.

It was the same as the judge called the name of the second place winner, a rather chubby little girl who seemed not to do anything but smile any day of the week, which the boy had always found to be most annoying.

And there it was, his long-awaited moment of recognition and glory. The judge waited for the crowd to settle after the smiling girl went back to her place before he began to speak.

"And in first place," he said, as the boy began to move toward him, "Sheila Pinkham!!"

The stunned boy stopped in his tracks, the smug smile becoming a look of horror, which turned quickly to one of embarrassment, then anger, and finally outrage. Everything was in slow motion, as the blood rushed past his ears and the sounds of the cheering crowd faded into nothingness.

He turned and ran as fast as his legs would carry him. He did not know where he was going, nor did he care. He just had to run. And before long, the tears of humiliation streaming down his face, he had put quite a bit of distance between himself and those horribly stupid judges. He wanted to leave the feelings of inadequacy behind as well, but when he finally stopped running, panting hard and falling to the ground, he found that they had followed him. And he knew in that moment that they would be with him wherever he went, until he was very famous and very rich.

The boy lay there for a long time, in the middle of an empty field, where no one could see him, or hear his heartbroken sobs. He cried until he could cry no longer, tears of hurt, of frustration and jealousy. And what made the whole situation worse was how awful he thought Sheila Pinkham was to begin with! She was a scrawny, pale, whiney little thing, with lots of allergies, and she was always sniffling and blowing her nose. She was about the most annoying girl in the whole school! How on earth could those judges pick her over him? And that painting that they thought was so wonderful -- hah! He had more artistic ability in his little finger than she would ever have in a lifetime. Those judges obviously had no idea what they were doing, and most certainly, they were not qualified for the job. The more he thought about the entire issue, the more disgusted he became.

His shame and humiliation fed his anger and jealousy, mighty beasts that they were becoming. They grew inside him like a fire raging out of control, and soon, he was able to pick himself up and slowly make his way home. By then, it was getting dark. His parents had been very worried about him, and he struggled to tell them what had happened. He had been so certain he would win, and it made him sick to think that he had to come home without any ribbon at all.

Of course, his parents were not concerned about whether or not he had won; they loved him just the same. But they well understood how terribly disappointed and upset their son was feeling. They tried, unsuccessfully, to console him. There was nothing they could say that even slightly diminished his rage or his shame.

He was very quiet that evening, and for a long time afterward. He seemed to have retreated into himself completely, and he began to work harder at finding odd jobs, in order to buy more paints and canvas. Every penny he earned went toward art supplies, and he became driven in a way his parents had never seen before. When he was not working at earning money, he was working on his paintings. He began to sleep very little, determined to create art that was going to make him rich beyond his wildest imaginings.

When he did sleep, he was always restless, thrashing around in his small bed, becoming tangled in the sheets. He began to have one particular dream with great regularity, a dream that he could never quite remember, but one that always caused him to wake with a start, drenched in sweat.

All he could ever remember of this dream was that it was very dark, and there was an eerie figure that seemed to be beckoning, calling to him, with a bony, claw-like hand that stretched out to him from the folds of a long, black cloak. There were never any words spoken, and he could not make out the face, but there was no mistaking the feeling in this dream. It was ominous, terrifying, and felt very, very real. And the worst part was that this dream occurred frequently for many long years.

The parents became worried about their pale and exhausted son, but every attempt to express their concern was met with an angry retort, with the boy storming off to his room, slamming the door behind him as he headed for his paints.

The years passed and the boy's parents died. His father had not seen the boy reach adulthood, his health having been poor for much of the child's life. His mother finally succumbed to disease caused by poverty. The strain of such worry, and an inadequate diet finally took their toll. And when she died, the boy, then a young man, sold the family's home and moved to a run-down little cottage at the edge of a remote and tiny village. In doing so, he was able to save most of the money he received from the sale of the house, and he could devote his days to his beloved painting.

He was happy to have a little nest egg, and he was certain that he would make a good living, selling his paintings in this new village. Soon, word would spread of this great artist's creations, and people would be flocking to him from miles around. He needed to be ready with a good supply, so he set to work, painting day and night.

It was not often that anyone passed by his cottage, due to the location, and to the fact that there were not many people in the village anyway. But when anyone did happen along the path on a sunny day, the artist could be seen in the garden, busily creating his paintings where he was certain villagers would be enticed to buy them. When it rained, he moved himself indoors and continued.

He had heard about some very famous artists whose work was selling for exorbitant prices, and he was desperate to be counted amongst them. He barely ate or slept, so he could paint and paint and paint. But as much as he painted, his artwork never improved. In fact, the more desperate and miserly he became, the worse his paintings were.

Many times, people who passed by called out a word of greeting to the artist. If he replied at all, it was without looking up from his work, and it was more of a growl than anything. "Do you want to buy a painting?" he would bark. But no one ever did.

Occasionally, someone would try to strike up a friendly conversation, or ask if he would like to visit them for a cup of tea, but he would turn them away, gruffly telling them that he could not be bothered, and saying that he was busy creating masterpieces that would make him rich and famous. To him, friends were a waste of his valuable creating time.

On occasion, there would be a knock at the door, with someone on the other side of it needing his help. And on every occasion, he would bark through the closed door, "Go away! Unless you want to buy a painting, don't bother me!" irritated that anyone would interrupt his creative process.

After a while, people stopped calling to him as they passed, and there were no more offers of friendship. And most certainly, no one came looking for help. The artist had finally made it clear that he wanted nothing to do with any of the villagers. He had all the peace and quiet he wanted and he painted to his heart's content.

In time, his little cottage was bursting at the seams, for it could no longer contain all of his paintings. He could not understand why no one would buy them; after all, they were so beautiful! The people in the village knew he was a very busy artist; they saw him outside painting often enough. So why, then, did no one was stop in to have a look and take one home, leaving lots of their money in his hands? Becoming quite disgusted with the stupidity of the villagers, his frustration and anger grew, along with his ever-increasing desire to be rich and famous.

There he was, with a vast collection of his art, and it was not moving. Still, he continued to buy lots of paints and many rolls of canvas, and he kept creating. His nest egg began to dwindle, as he had not yet begun to earn anything from what he believed to be his God-given talent and destiny.

Eventually, the man was just about out of money. His plan had gone awry. He had long since begun eating very little, trying to make his money last as long as possible. When it came down to a choice between food and art supplies, he opted for very little food, determined to have the best possible selection of paintings for his customers to view. He was certain that one day soon, that first buyer was going to knock on his door, and he needed to be ready for the swarms of people who were sure to follow.

With such a poor diet, and with only a tiny bit of rest each night, it was not long before his health began to fail. Always a very miserly man, as the number of coins in his jar dwindled, he became even more fearful and obsessed with needing enough money to support several kingdoms.

Late one stormy evening, the man was busily painting yet another picture by the light of one lonely little candle. Lightning flashed, lighting up the night sky, while deafening cracks of thunder fairly shook the little cottage. He barely seemed to notice the raging storm, in all likelihood because it matched his mood. As the wind howled, and whistled through the cracks in the cottage, suddenly he had the strangest sensation that he was not alone. Certain that there were unseen eyes fixing their gaze upon him, the hairs on the back of his neck stood straight up.

He stopped painting, listening intently, afraid to move. Fear gripped his heart when he thought he heard a quiet, rasping sigh. Swallowing hard, his throat suddenly very dry, slowly he turned around. As he scanned the darkened room, his stomach churned and seemed to drop to his knees when there, in the shadows, he saw the vague outline of a cloaked figure.

He choked back a scream that he was certain would have been bloodcurdling, had it escaped from his tight, dry throat. It could not be! This was his nightmare, come to life! Terror filled every part of his being, from every cell of his body, straight through to the center of his soul.

Struggling not to show his fear, he mustered all the courage he could, but his fright was obvious as he called out nervously, "Who are you? What do you want?!

Silence was his only reply.

"How did you get in here? I'm warning you, get out of here immediately!" His terror was unmistakable; all efforts to mask it were futile.

The figure moved slightly, but toward him and out of the shadows just a little; there was no evidence of an impending retreat. He had not thought it possible to be any more terrified than he was already, but this little movement proved him to be wrong.

The artist became more frightened still, on realising that he was not at all threatening to this intruder, whose eerie presence caused his blood to run cold, chilling him to the bone.

The only sounds the artist could now hear were his own heart pounding in his chest, and the blood rushing past his ears. Once again, the figure edged a little closer to him, and he heard the quiet rustle of the cloak, swishing across the floor.

Still, there was not a word from his unwelcome guest, who moved ever closer and into the dim light of the flickering candle.

The artist's heart beat wildly in his chest; his breath was shallow and ragged. His mind raced as he struggled to find a way to end this nightmare.

And then, the figure stepped forward, moving out of the shadows. The artist saw an ugly, old woman, the hood of her black cloak loosely covering long, stringy, gray strands of hair, her face contorted and terrifying, the colour of Death.

"What do you want from me?" the artist demanded, his mouth as dry as the desert sand at mid-day.

The crone was silent for a moment. And when she began to speak, the hair on the back of the artist's neck once again stood on end, her low and raspy voice causing him to shudder.

"I have come to give you all you have worked for, to see that you get exactly what you have earned."

The Spirit Within

The man was puzzled. All he had worked for? Fame and fortune were all he wanted, but how could this terrifying and broken old crone give him these?

"Wh-wh-what do you mean?" he stammered in confusion and fear.

"I mean exactly what I said. I have come to grant your wishes," was the quiet reply, that horrible voice, making the man shudder.

The artist's fear began to leave him, as thoughts and images of wealth and notoriety flooded into his mind.

"And how will you do that?" he asked, suspicious of her statements.

"You will see. But first, you must promise that one day, you will do something for me."

The man thought for a moment, suddenly not quite as excited about the proposition. After all, he had never had any interest in helping anyone at all, other than himself.

"And just what is it that you would have me do?" he queried, somewhat defiantly - and suspiciously.

"That remains to be seen. It will be one request, one time, but I know not what it will be, or when I will ask. In return, you will have fame and wealth beyond your wildest imaginings, just as you have always desired."

The man pondered the crone's words for a few moments. His money was about to run out, it was true, and certainly, he was not selling any of his paintings, although he could not understand why. He decided that with fame and fortune, he would have enough people working for him, and enough money behind him, that anything the old woman could ever ask in the future would be easily managed, so it seemed a fair exchange.

"All right," he said firmly. "I will agree to your terms."

A little draft rushed past the back of the man's neck, causing a chill that was most disconcerting.

The crone reached deep into a black, drawstring bag, and pulled out a glass bottle with an old cork stuffed in its neck. With her bony hand, she held it out to the man, as he vividly recalled the claw-like fingers in his dream.

"What's this?" he asked, reaching hesitantly for it, afraid to touch her dry and withered skin.

"It is a Transformation Potion," the old woman replied. "Put a drop on yourself and you will be seen as the most gifted artist who ever lived. Then put a drop on each of your paintings, and everyone will think they are beautiful works of art. No one will be able to resist buying them, no matter what the cost."

The man was most insulted by these remarks. His hand shot back from the bottle. "How dare you, Old Woman?!" he exclaimed, with great indignation. "I *am* a very gifted artist, and my paintings *are* beautiful works of art!"

"You are wrong, sir, on both counts, but I am not here to argue either point. Simply do as I tell you, and very soon, you will receive all you deserve. And remember our agreement. One day, I shall return to make a request of you, and you shall do as I ask."

Offended, yet eager for his wishes to be granted, the man decided to let the crone's comments pass without further debate. It was more important for him to have all the money he could possibly imagine than it was for him to waste valuable time convincing this foolish old hag that she was wrong.

With a look on his face that bordered on disgust, the artist snatched the bottle out of the old woman's gnarled hand. Turning his attention to it, and staring at the glass, he wondered how soon he would be rich. He looked up to ask the crone this question, but she had vanished without a sound.

That night, the artist did not sleep. Instead, he thrashed around in his bed, contemplating his future, and anxious to be wealthy and famous. As the sun rose, it found him out of his bed, having a very early start to his day, eager to reap the rewards of all his hard work. With the daylight, he was better able to reach all of his paintings, stacked and buried in his cottage, and put a drop of the transformation potion on each.

Once he had completed his task, very carefully, he put a drop on himself. A tingle ran through his body, like a little electrical charge. It disappeared after a few moments, and the artist was somewhat disappointed when nothing else happened. He hoped he had not been duped, and was readying himself to find the old crone and have it out with her if nothing came of this.

He did not have to wait long, however, to see that she had been true to her word. Before most people would have even sat down to breakfast, there were knocks upon the door, with people on the other side, asking if they could please see his paintings. He was all smiles, as he waved them in, and, oh, how he delighted in hearing them oooh and aaaah at his creations.

Over the following days, his previously bulging little cottage was gradually emptying, as more and more people came, anxious to purchase his paintings. They could not seem to buy them fast enough, and as supplies dwindled, customers began to fight with each other over the paintings. The artist took advantage of this supply and demand problem. He put the prices up, higher and higher. Still, the people came, and still they bought, just as fast.

The more they bought, the faster he raised the prices. The cost did not seem to matter to his customers; they had to have his paintings, just as the crone had told him would happen. Some were even heard discussing how it was going to create serious financial hardship for them, yet they seemed driven to purchase his paintings, despite the consequences. He could not have cared less that these people were using their food money, and lots of it, to buy his art. Instead, as he listened to those discussions, all he gathered was that he must be an amazing artist to cause people to go to such lengths to own one of his paintings.

Soon, every one of them was gone, and he had several large sacks of money hidden under his bed. He could not believe his eyes. Finally, he was able to purchase more art supplies, and better ones, and he set about the business of creating many more paintings, turning away countless disappointed people, who promised they would return when he had replenished his supply.

Day after day, there were long queues of customers, who waited outside his cottage, desperate for him to finish a painting and then fighting each other for it, offering higher and higher prices which very quickly brought fame and wealth to the greedy artist.

News of his incredible talent and paintings spread like wildfire, and soon, the man had moved to a beautiful castle, high on a hill, overlooking the sea. He had more servants than he could ever possibly need. Many of them had no real work to do, but the artist enjoyed being able to tell everyone how many he required. It impressed people, making him feel very important and superior.

Although the man already had far more money than he could ever use, his greed and ambition did not diminish. In fact, they grew. The more money he had, the more he thought he needed. Day and night, he continued to paint, barely stopping to eat. He continued to put increasingly ridiculous prices on his paintings, along with a little of the Transformation Potion, of course, and people who could ill afford them still flocked to his castle, putting themselves in dire financial straits just to own his creations. The artist would only laugh and rub his hands together with glee when he saw them coming, utterly delight and excited about taking all their money before they left.

One day, the artist was on a castle balcony, painting the ocean view from his lofty position. It was a lovely, sunny day, and the water was a particularly brilliant shade of blue. He loved listening to the waves, crashing into the shore, amidst the cries of the gulls as they swooped and soared overhead. A delicate breeze played with the leaves on the trees, creating a soft, rustling sound, which was somewhat soothing to the man who lived with constant anxiety. It was the first time he could remember feeling any sort of love or appreciation for the beauty around him. Although it was a strange feeling, it warmed his heart, and gave him a sense of peace that was entirely unfamiliar to him.

As he stared out at the lovely scene below him, he noticed in the distance a young woman, walking alone along the cliffs. Curious about her, he stopped painting, holding his brush in mid-air while he stood transfixed. Her movements were unhurried, and she paused frequently to look out over the water for a few moments before walking a little further.

Eventually, she climbed up on a rather large rock, and seated herself so that she was facing the ocean. The sea breeze played with her long, flowing hair, and holding her face to the sun, she leaned back on her hands, feet dangling high above the water.

The artist was smitten, even though he could not even see the woman clearly. She was near enough for him to know that she was very beautiful, but too far away to be seen distinctly. He stood, mesmerised for some time.

Suddenly, he found himself leaving his paints and brushes, and dashing through the castle halls, tearing down stairways, and racing across the grounds. Once on the other side of the wall, he hurried along the shore of the ocean, until he had the woman in his sight. Composing himself, he ran his fingers through his hair, straightened his clothes, and tried to hide his nervousness as he sauntered toward her, a slight stagger in his gait, as he overcompensated for his anxiety by trying extra hard to look as though he were quite confident.

The woman had not moved in some time. She was still sitting on the rock, leaning back on her hands, face to the sun, when he had got within several feet of her. He could see that her eyes were closed, but he was certain that she should have been able to hear him approaching on the rocks, yet she seemed unaware of his presence.

He faltered, wondering whether he should interrupt her obvious deep thoughts, wondering whether he was intruding, wondering whether he should turn back and run from her. He had no experience with women, having been consumed by his burning need to paint and become wealthy, so he was entirely lost.

As he stood in his place, staring at the beauty before him, and wondering what he should next do, he was startled when the woman suddenly spoke. Without opening her eyes or moving, she simply said, "Come, sit here beside me."

The artist was more than a little surprised by this; she had not even seen the person who had intruded on her peaceful afternoon. Without a word, he climbed up on the rock, and then hesitated, wondering just how much distance he should leave between himself and the woman.

"Right beside me," she directed, as though she had read his

thoughts. It was more than a little strange, and was somewhat disconcerting, yet he did not question her, and instead, he merely complied.

"You live in the castle," she stated; she was not asking.

Once again, the artist felt a little uncomfortable with her manner, but simply responded, "Uh, yes. Yes, I do. How did you know?"

She laughed, tossing her head back, and then turned to him, finally opening her eyes and looking at the man she had invited to sit beside her. "Are you not a famous and wealthy artist? Everyone knows where you live. And no one else lives out here."

"Ah." There was something about her that left him feeling unclothed, as if she could see right through him. He felt exposed and worried about what she might find.

The two sat and talked for a while, she in her wisdom, he in his nervousness, and after a time, he felt brave enough to invite her to the castle for a drink and a meal. She was only too happy to agree, which surprised and delighted the artist, and they walked back together as the sun was beginning to sink into the ocean.

After the two had shared a lovely meal that evening, the artist took the woman to his studio, and showed her his paintings. Having used the Transformation Potion for so long, he was used to people being extremely impressed with his work, and he had forgotten that it was the potion that created this reaction, and not actually his art.

As they walked through the open door, they were immediately faced with numerous paintings hanging on the walls, or standing on easels. Every piece of art was bland, boring, and miserable with muddy colours, one blending into the next, just as the paintings did. Yet the artist was filled with pride, beaming and waiting for the usual reaction that he got from viewers.

But this time it was different. The woman did not say much about any of them; in fact, she seemed entirely unimpressed. She wore a rather bored expression, and attempted to be polite.

The artist felt panic arising from his stomach. He was not particularly concerned with her opinion of his work; he was so smitten with her, it didn't matter if she detested everything he created. What if the potion was wearing off? What if no one wanted to buy - or even see - his work any more? What if he never sold another painting? Yes, it was true that he had a ridiculous amount of money, but one could never have too much - just in case - and he was not at all prepared to stop earning it already!

Hiding his concerns about the potion and the money, he continued to have a wonderful evening with the woman, until it was time for her to take her leave. He called for a servant to prepare a coach and horses, but she insisted that she would find her own way home.

"Please, it's the least I can do to see that you arrive home safely!" he offered, concerned for someone else's well being for the first time in his life.

"No. Thank you very much. I prefer it this way." Something about her made him aware that he must remain silent and accept her decision.

It was a sweet parting that evening, both the artist and the woman expressing their desire to see each other again soon.

The artist simply could not believe his good fortune. This woman seemed to touch a part of his soul that he had not known existed, and it was wonderful.

The two spent a lot of time together in the weeks that followed; for the first time in many years, the artist took a break from his round-the-clock painting, which had become a lifestyle. His anxiety about money had not dissipated by any means, but this wonderful new relationship distracted him from worrying excessively.

But from time to time, fearful thoughts of the potion's failure rolled through his mind. Not wanting to face rejection or criticism of his work, he stopped allowing customers in, informing his staff to say he was on holiday.

It did not take the artist and the woman to become close and frequent companions. It was one night, over a beautiful, candlelit dinner on the balcony, overlooking the last remnants of a striking sunset, so stunningly reflected in the sea, that the artist was brave enough to propose marriage.

For all the confidence he had with his paintings, certainly he had none with women. Really, he thought himself quite bold to dare to ask such a lovely young woman for her hand in marriage. Deep in his heart, he did not believe that he deserved such a wife, but certainly he would not want to admit this to anyone, not with his position in society! How delighted he was, when she agreed to become his wife.

Because of his ongoing anxiety about money, he was rather afraid to bring up the subject of their wedding. He was torn between wanting to have a very lavish one, if that was what she wanted, and knowing that the potion may no longer be working, which would prevent him from earning much more money. He was very happy, however, when almost as if she'd been reading his mind, she broached the subject with him, telling him that she really wanted a very private, quiet affair.

He tried to hide his relief about her decision, but did the polite and appropriate thing, asking her if she was absolutely certain. "After all, my love," he said, "This will be your only wedding, and it must be as you wish."

She smiled and nodded gently, reassuring him that it was, in fact, as she wished.

They did not waste any time in seeing to the simple arrangements, and before long, they were standing together on the rock where they met by the sea, proclaiming their love for one another, and becoming husband and wife.

It was a magical day; the artist forgot his worries and his ambitions for much of it, simply delighting in the joy of having this lovely young woman become his wife. It was the happiest day of his life. In fact, when he looked back over his years right the way back to childhood, he realised that he had never known happiness at all until he met her.

The two seemed well suited to each other; he was not much of a conversationalist, never having spent much time around people, and she was very quiet. Both seemed content with the long silences between them. They simply enjoyed being together. He began to paint again, and she would often sit in the room with him, reading, or otherwise occupying herself, while he created his works of art.

After a brief honeymoon period, the artist once again prepared to open his doors to prospective buyers of his paintings. Nervously, as the first lot lined up outside, he paced back and forth in the studio, afraid that the potion was no longer working. His anxiety mounted by the minute, until finally, he could stand it no longer. He had to know.

He stopped in his tracks, staring at the door, bracing himself for the worst possible outcome. Drawing in a very deep breath, he marched toward the door and opened it, as if somehow, pretending to be brave might alter the situation.

In they filed, one at a time, having heard of this very great artist and his magnificent work. The man scarcely took a breath as he watched them moving amongst his paintings, biting his lip as he waited to hear the response.

At last, there were the familiar 'ooohs' and 'aaaahs' to which he had become accustomed, and his customers began to make their selections, still paying unbelievably outrageous prices for his work.

'Ah,' he thought, 'All is right in my world.' But then, another thought struck him, and it felt like a bucket of cold water, emptied directly on his head. He was always in such a rush to put the potion on the paintings, so that he could hang and sell them, it had been quite some time since he had bothered to check to see how much of it remained. He had always known the bottle would someday be emptied, but as long as the money was pouring in like the water rushing over Niagara Falls, he had not given it much thought.

As the sun poured through the castle window, the artist slipped away from his customers for a few moments into a little room off the studio, and fetched the bottle of Transformation Potion from its secret hiding place in the stone wall. He was stunned to notice that it was almost empty! He had not realised that the potion was disappearing, although when he thought about it, he was amazed that it has lasted all those years.

Remembering the poverty and humiliation with which he grew up, he felt a sudden resurgence of his boyhood fears welling up in his stomach and rising to his throat.

'Well,' he thought to himself, 'I have no choice but to charge even more exorbitant prices for my work while I still have some of this potion.' And that is exactly what he did.

The miserly artist soon seemed to forget how smitten he had been with his lovely bride, and he spent more and more time painting, returning to his old habit of creating day and night. The more he painted and used up the potion, the more anxious he became. The more anxious he became, the more he painted and used up the potion.

Rapidly, his wife grew bored watching her frantic and desperate husband at the easel every waking minute. Many times, she tried to speak with him, only getting a distracted grunt or 'hm' in response. Eventually, he did not even seem to notice when she entered the room.

Late one winter's night, as the artist stood at his easel, painting again by the light of one small candle in an effort to conserve money, he was suddenly struck by the feeling that he was not alone, that he was being watched.

Instantly, he recalled the night the old crone appeared in his little cottage. As the hair on the back of his neck stood on end once again, he was quite certain that this was the moment he had once dreaded, but had long since put out of his head.

Slowly turning around, there, in the shadows, was a cloaked figure, silent and unmoving.

This time, the artist was not so afraid, yet he was nervous about what might be asked of him. "Come out of the shadows, Old Woman! Show yourself!" he commanded.

After a moment or two, the crone stepped into the dim and flickering light of the candle. The two faced each other, recalling their first meeting.

Finally, the old hag spoke. "I have come with my request. As you well know, I honoured my promise to give you everything you deserved, and now it is your turn to honour yours. Are you ready to do as I ask?"

Nervously, the man swallowed and replied, "Yes. Hurry up with it, then. You are wasting my time."

His curt reply seemed to annoy the old woman, as a look of disdain crossed her twisted face.

"There is a little boy who needs your help. His parents are dead and he has no means of supporting himself. He is a very gifted artist, but cannot afford food, much less paints and canvas. He huddles in doorways at night without even a blanket to protect him from the elements and he eats only if he can find anything others have thrown away. You will give him some money, keeping him fed, sheltered, and painting."

"That is preposterous!" he cried indignantly. "I cannot afford to support someone else! What if I run out of money? And if this snot-nosed little kid is so talented, he will be my rival! Why should I help a competitor, someone who could take sales away from me, and especially as I am running out of the potion!"

He was certainly not going to be responsible for his own fall from the pedestal upon which he had been placed. It was true, he believed he deserved to be there. In reality, it was magic that had created the situation, yet he did not wish to acknowledge this.

He took a few moments to consider the old woman's request, and then flatly refused to comply. Her dark eyes flashed in anger, her thin lips were pressed together in a stern line.

"You have almost run out of the Transformation Potion. Does this not concern you?" she asked, knowingly.

"Of course not!" he lied, growing more nervous. "And just how would you know how much I have left? For all you know, I may have run out long ago!"

She cackled, sneering at the suggestion that anyone would buy his paintings without the help of her magic. "I know that no one would buy any of your work, unless you had applied the potion. Have you forgotten your little cottage that was bursting at the seams because no one even looked at your dreadful paintings? You will not sell one more when the potion runs out."

The artist's anxiety ripped through his stomach and flew directly to his heart, clutching at it with desperation. But of course, he did not want the old crone to see this.

As calmly as he could manage, he squinted directly into her ugly, beady little eyes. "You will see that you are wrong. I have an excellent reputation. Everyone knows that I am the greatest artist who ever lived, and they will still want to buy my paintings, just to say they own my work, even if they do not like it. That is what people do, so my future is quite safe. I no longer need your potion," he shouted, desperate to believe the lie.

The old woman's eyes flashed again. Giving him a moment to allow his discomfort to grow, she rather enjoyed watching him attempt to hide it.

"And what is your answer, then, about the boy?" she queried.

"I have given you my answer. Ask me for something else, but I refuse to part with my money, and I most certainly will not promote a child who could oust me from my current position. He will have to find his own way; his problems are none of my concern."

The crone stood in silence for a few moments, and then asked, "Are you quite certain that this is your answer? You do not wish to reconsider?"

"Yes, that is my answer, and I will not reconsider," he replied, emphatically. "You are asking far too much of me."

The old hag contemplated reminding him of what she had done for him, but well knew the comment would be lost on him entirely. Rather, she simply stated, "I always keep my promises."

And with that, she vanished before his eyes.

The artist stood in silence for a moment, wondering whether there might be some consequence for his refusal of her request. He had not thought to ask her this; it had not occurred to him as she stood before him. His only thought had been for his money. Nervously, he turned back to his painting, unsuccessfully trying to shake off the nagging feeling that he had not yet seen the last of the crone.

Once again, the man had a very restless night after his visit from the old woman. He tossed and turned, thrashed and fretted until the wee hours, when he finally dozed off, exhausted from worry.

A couple of hours later, the man awoke, and with still-closed eyes, was aware of sunlight pouring into the room. It took a few seconds before the events of the previous night flooded back into his memory, and with them, came the anxiety. Upon opening his eyes and focusing on the room around him, he sat bolt upright in horror! "No!" he screamed aloud. "This must be another nightmare!" Shutting his eyes hard and shaking his head, he tried to convince himself that what he saw could not possibly be real.

Opening his eyes once more, he saw that he was sitting in bed in his cramped, run-down little cottage. Everything was exactly as it had been on that night so many years before, that night the old crone had come to call. He was horrified! What was happening? How could this be? Where was his wife? A million questions ripped through his mind like daggers, as he tried to understand.

He crept out of bed and wandered through the tiny cottage, seeing everything exactly as he remembered it being on the night that the old crone had come to him. There were a few bits of bread in the cupboard, several nearly-empty tubes of paint, his worn, old brushes, the one small piece of candle, and of course, a few pennies in the jar. The only difference was that the paintings were all gone.

After a few moments' silence, as the artist struggled to absorb the shock of this rude awakening, he suddenly let out one long, tormented scream, before collapsing on the floor in tears.

The days passed. The man's hair had turned completely white from shock, and he had fallen into a state of ill health from fear and starvation. He wished that he had some supplies so that he could begin painting again, believing that he could earn a living. "After all," he said out loud, "People used to love... my..."

His voice trailed off, suddenly hit with the knowledge that the crone had been right; they had only loved his paintings because of the Transformation Potion. Of course he'd known it all along, but denial is a wonderful thing. Throughout those years, he enjoyed the fantasy, pretending that he was truly a gifted artist. But he could pretend no more.

And in that moment, as much as he thought his whole world has already fallen apart, it came crashing down around his ears with the knowledge that he was not, and never would be an artist. All his childhood fears of starvation and poverty had now become a living nightmare. His attempts to relieve his greatest fears had only brought him more of the same. It was too much to bear. In the blink of an eye, a lifetime of dreams and ambitions lay shattered and in pieces around him.

The Spirit Within

Every part of him was crushed, smashed, absolutely blown to pieces. He had only ever had one dream, and that was to become a magnificent artist. Never had he considered any other career. He was trained in nothing, and had only ever done odd jobs to earn money. He had no idea what his future held. It was as barren, black and empty as it could possibly be.

And his beloved wife was gone, too.

At that moment, he wished desperately that he would just die. He believed that he could not be so lucky, however; he was certain that he had no right to die and escape his misery. He had been such a fool, such a hateful and selfish fool. And now he must reap the rewards of such a lifetime.

It was dreadfully cold and biting outside that winter. With no fuel for the fire, it was not much warmer in his cottage, but at least he was protected from the wind and the snow.

He had never known hunger like this. His belly ached from morning till night, and he felt increasingly weak and ill. He coughed incessantly, making it impossible to rest or get well. One night, he felt he could stand it no more. He was desperate for food, and maybe a few logs for his fire. Wrapping himself in an old, thin coat, his only protection from the harsh night air, he stumbled outside and down the road.

Knocking on doors, he begged for help. Several concerned faces appeared as doors were opened to him, but the concern quickly became disgust, anger or resentment when the villagers realised who needed their assistance. The doors would soon be closed, sometimes with a few unkind words, other times with complete silence.

He began to recall the many times someone had knocked on his door, offering friendship or asking for help. And for the first time in his life, he knew remorse and compassion. As he trudged on, stooped over, head down against the wind, hoping to find just one kind soul who would be willing to help him, he wept, overcome with shame. The tears froze on his icy cheeks, but he did not notice; he was consumed by his guilt.

Stumbling along through the wind and snow, the artist reviewed his life and his choices. He saw that he had been exceedingly selfish and greedy, that he had never cared about another living soul, except for his young wife. Sadly, he realized that even with her, with his beautiful bride, he had taken her for granted, and had once again allowed his selfishness to rule his life. He did not deserve her.

The crone had been right. She kept her promises. And she had given him exactly what he deserved, just as she said she would do.

He thought about how he had used magic to sell his paintings, and even worse, that he had been paid ridiculous sums of money for them, which often caused serious financial hardship for people. It ruined many lives and created the same kind of poverty for them that he had detested enduring as a child.

His own experience with hunger and fear for his survival and future were only the tiniest glimpse into what he had done to countless people through the years. And all the while, he had cared only about himself and his money. One after another, his sins and his failings came to him, slamming into his head and his heart, creating such torment that he could bear it no longer.

At that moment, he collapsed in the snow, sobbing loudly but uncaring, as he finally understood just what kind of man he had been all those years.

Not far from where he lay frozen and starving in the snow, there was a tiny little cottage. The flickering firelight in the window was warm and inviting. But the artist did not see it.

Inside the cottage, a woman and her three young sons were preparing to have their sparse evening meal. They were awfully thin, and their clothes were all in tatters. One of the children suddenly cried, "Did you hear that?!" Everyone was silent. They could hear only the howling and whistling of the wind.

But then, there was something else. "There!" he cried, "There it is again!" They listened a little harder, the mother going to the window and peering outside.

The little boy said, "It sounds like someone crying, Mother!"

As she looked outside, the mother thought she saw a crumpled figure, lying in the snow.

"Quickly!" she said to the two older boys. "Fetch your coats and get him inside!"

The boys did as they were told, and in a couple of minutes, they had managed to help the man stumble into the warmth of their tiny cottage, his head hanging, not entirely aware of what was happening around him.

They sat him in a chair by the fire, and it was then that the woman saw who he was. He did not see the look on her face, and it was just as well, given his current condition, and all that he had just come to understand.

The woman said not a word, but promptly drew some steaming water from a kettle in the fireplace, and made a cup of tea for the man. She covered him with two thin blankets, tucking them in around him, and lifted his feet onto the hearth. By the time he had sipped at his tea, and had been warmed by the fire, he had composed himself a little. Looking up at the woman, standing beside him, his eyes filled with tears. Choking on the lump in his throat, with great humility, he thanked her.

She made no reply, nor did she smile at him, but rather, she turned and gathered the children around the table. Retrieving a pot of very thin soup from the fireplace, she set it on the table, and set out a small amount of bread on a plate next to it. After ladelling out a portion of the soup for each child, she put the last of it into a bowl, took a small piece of the bread, and offered these to the man. Incredulous, he stared at her, at her offering, and at the table, realising that there was no more food for herself.

"No, please, you are very kind, but that is the last of your food. I cannot accept it."

She stood silently over him, still offering the bowl and the bread. Once again he politely refused, feeling even more guilt and shame than he had whilst he lay out in the snow.

Placing the bowl and the bread on a tiny table next to his chair, she said, "Please. Eat. It is not much, but it is all I have to offer, and you need it far more than I."

He looked at the tattered clothing on the family's thin bodies, and realised the enormity of this gift. He knew he was entirely undeserving, but the woman was insistent.

At last, too weak from hunger, from cold, and from emotion, he sipped at one spoonful of the soup after another, until it was gone. It was mostly broth, but it was the best meal he had ever eaten. Just before he had come inside this beautiful little cottage, he was certain he was just moments from Death, which would have been a blessed relief at that time. And now, with each spoonful of soup, he felt Life returning, coursing through his veins, both body and soul being nourished by the woman's most generous gift.

After he had finished the meager meal, the woman noticed that he had a little colour in his face. He was drawn and haggard, and his hair was entirely white, but there was no mistaking who he was. She mustered her courage and asked him, "Do you know who I am?"

He studied her face, believing that her query meant he should be able to answer, 'Yes.' But he could not. Immediately, he felt shame. So many faces in the village, so many people lived right near him for much of his life, yet he knew no one.

"I'm so sorry, Ma'am, but no, I do not know you."

"I thought not," was her simple reply, wearing an expression that he could not begin to describe. "My husband and I knocked on your door, wanting to befriend you on several occasions, but you always turned us away. Eventually, we had decided not to return, as quite clearly, you had no interest.

"But suddenly one day, my husband and I were compelled to go to you for one of your paintings," she continued. "It was an exorbitant amount of money, costing every bit of our savings.

"It was the strangest thing. It was as though we were under a spell. We both knew that it was entirely wrong, that we had children to feed, and bills to pay, yet it was as though something was forcing us to buy your painting, even though we knew it was a terrible idea. It was as though we had no choice, no will of our own."

She grew silent for a moment, and the man felt even more shame and guilt wash over him than before. He could find no words inside himself, only raw emotion.

"Soon after we bought the painting, it was as though we were cursed. Our tiny daughter, a very healthy and robust wee girl, suddenly became very ill and died. Immediately after that, my husband lost his job and could not find another. We struggled to keep our family fed and warm. And then, with all the strain and guilt, my husband fell into such a deep depression that he took his own life."

The artist sat in stunned silence, not having any idea what he could possibly say to this woman, and feeling entirely responsible for every bit of her loss and her pain. Once again, the tears began to fall.

As she continued her story, her voice changed and became quietly angry. "After my husband died, I felt more certain than ever that the painting was cursed. I could not wait to be rid of it. In a fit of rage and grief one night, I tore it down from the wall, and smashed the frame, throwing the pieces and the canvas into the fire. I was certain that it had come from Hell, and I wanted it to go back there, far away from me and my sons."

The man could only weep in response, his face buried in his hands, as he cried, "I'm sorry! I'm sorry! I'm so sorry!" over and over again.

"Many times, I heard countless similar stories from other villagers for a long time after you left to live in your big castle. Your paintings, sir, have brought nothing but hardship and misery to their owners."

The woman left him to his remorse and the room fell quiet, except for the man's sobs, which gradually subsided until he was entirely spent. The woman just sat opposite him, rocking by the fire and staring into it, a million miles away and lost in her grief.

A little while later, the woman refilled the man's tea, and made some for herself and the children, then returned to her chair. The two sat in silence for some time, until the woman spoke, telling her children it was time for bed. After goodnight kisses between mother and sons, the boys disappeared to their tiny bedroom.

Alone for the first time that evening, the silence grew awkward. Realising that it was time to leave, but struggling to find the right words to say, he stood, clearing his throat. Wrapping his thin coat tightly around himself before heading back into the cold, he turned to face the woman.

"I have to ask you," the man said, hesitating for a moment. "After all you have been through because you bought my painting, and after how unbearably rude I had been to you in the past, why did you take me in and treat me with such kindness?"

"It is simple," she said. "You needed my help."

"But I do not deserve it!" he cried.

"Of course you do. We all make mistakes. We all deserve forgiveness. And what is the point of being on this earth, if not to help one another?"

The artist was overcome with emotion. Choking back more tears, he offered the woman a warm hug, knowing no other way to express what was in his heart. She accepted it, and after he thanked her profusely, she sent him on his way with a few logs under his arm, and a little packet of nuts and dried fruit in his pocket.

The man had much to consider on his way home; he felt like a new man. His life was going to be very different, as different as it could possibly be.

The cottage was, of course, in darkness upon his return, yet the bright full moon shed enough light through the window that the man could see his way to the hearth. Quickly, he laid a fire, and as he struck a match to light the bit of paper under the logs, he was startled to see a pile of wood stacked neatly along the stone wall beside him. Bewildered, he tried to figure out who would have left him such a gift, and could find no answer to the question.

He sat there, on the floor, staring into the fire, contemplating many things, trying to find a place to begin to put his life right and to try to repair some of the damage he had caused. It was a most daunting task; he was completely overwhelmed.

Once the flames had warmed him, he stood and turned to face his tiny sitting room, which was bathed in the beautiful glow from the fire. As he moved across the room to hang up his coat and put away the woman's gifts of nuts and fruit, something caught his eye. Turning his head, he was stunned to see a basket of new brushes and tubes of paint, and a large roll of canvas, sitting on the table in a corner.

"What is this?" he wondered out loud in astonishment. "Who is leaving me these beautiful gifts, and why?"

Initially, upon seeing the painting supplies, he was thrilled and elated about being able to paint again. But his expression of joy suddenly turned to one of defeat, as his face fell, remembering that he was not an artist after all. Someone was taunting him. It could only be the crone.

He sank into a chair, wondering what should be done with these gifts, believing that he had no need of them, when suddenly, he noticed in the pit of his stomach, the tiniest seed of an old, familiar feeling. It was the desire to paint, and it was like the return of a long-lost friend. This was not manic desperation and frenzied need. But rather, this was what he remembered from when he a very small boy who just loved to paint, before it all went wrong for his parents.

It made him nervous, for he well remembered how it felt to have his dreams shattered before his very eyes, and he was not too eager to experience it again.

But something was different. The more he focused on the desire, the more it grew, until it seemed that it rose up from his stomach and into his heart, filling every part of his being with a burning need to create. Not for money. Not for fame. Just for the sake of it.

Despite the darkness in the room, the artist was compelled to stretch some canvas onto a frame and set it on his easel by the fire, where he had just enough light for painting. He was in a dreadful hurry to begin creating; he could not open the tubes of paint quickly enough, and squeeze dollops of beautiful colours onto the pallet. Grabbing his brushes, his hand flew from pallet to canvas and back again, applying broad, swift strokes as he worked.

Never had he felt anything like this before! It seemed that everything in his heart was flying straight down his arm, through the brush and onto the canvas. It was as though a dam had burst and every feeling he had ever stuffed, hidden or ignored came rushing out in a flood

He did not stop at one painting; he continued long into the night, until finally, the sun was coming up, lighting the room with the dawn of a new day. At last, he felt he could stop and take a breath. Standing back from the paintings that stood propped and drying around the room, in the morning light, he had his first good look at the fruits of his labour.

The artist was stunned beyond words. His eyes grew wide and his mouth fell open. He could truly say that these were, indeed, very beautiful works of art, completely unlike anything he had ever created in the past. They were full of life and emotion, passion and colour. In disbelief, he sank into a chair, exhausted, exhilarated, and weeping as he smiled, while he gazed at his incredible paintings.

He was not certain how long he had been asleep, but he awoke some time later, to discover that he had nodded off in his chair. In his sleepiness, before opening his eyes, he wondered if his night of painting had all been a dream, and was almost afraid to open his eyes. But open them he did. And there before him, still propped against walls and furniture, were his very beautiful creations.

Rising to stretch, stiff from his hours in the chair, the artist made his way across the room to have a closer look at each of his paintings. As he did so, he saw another basket, perched on the windowsill, and this one was filled with food. There were fruits and vegetables, a large piece of cheese, and a crusty loaf of bread.

Once again, he was astonished, puzzled about how these beautiful gifts had come to him, and who might have given them to him. His heart filled with wonder and gratitude, as he helped himself to some of the contents.

As the artist sat alone, enjoying his delicious meal, he gazed around the room at his creations and wondered what he would do with them. Certainly, no one would buy them after the life had previously led, but he was at peace with that knowledge, and decided he would try to give them away. Perhaps he could give them to a charity for an auction. It would have been wrong to attempt to sell them for himself, after how horribly selfish and greedy he had been in the past. He would find some other kind of work.

Of one thing, he was certain: he *__must__* paint. Whether or not anyone else ever saw one of his works of art again, he would continue to paint for the sake of self-expression, knowing that there was a piece of his soul in each of his creations.

During the night, the winter storm had passed, making way for a warmer, brighter day. Late in the afternoon, the artist went for a very long walk down the road and through the forest, taking the woman's packet of seeds and dried fruit along. He noticed his surroundings in a way that he never had before. The smell of the pine, the crunch of the snow under his feet, the little birds who searched for berries and seeds... he was especially touched by them, and felt compassion for the starving little birds and animals; he had become well-acquainted with how it felt to be hungry and to fear for one's own survival.

Although it was the only food he had, he was happy to reach into his pocket and pull out the packet that had been given to him the previous night. Scattering the nuts and seeds on the ground, he found himself wishing he could feed and help any living soul who was in need.

He stopped dead in his tracks. He remembered the young boy, the one the crone had asked him to help. Suddenly, he was filled with a great need to see if he could find this boy and offer him -- offer him what? He had nothing to give. He was not even certain about how he was going to be able to feed himself, much less look after a boy who was in as much need as that poor child was. His heart sank, momentarily having been so excited about having an opportunity to make a difference in the child's life, only to realise that he could do nothing.

Filled with shame and remorse, he hung his head as he continued to walk in the fading light of the setting sun. He could have done so much for the boy when he had all the riches of several kingdoms, had he not been so greedy and jealous. Thoroughly disgusted with himself for having left an innocent child to suffer, he could barely stand to think about it. Not only did that child deserve to have a home and food, he deserved the chance to become the artist that the crone said the boy was destined to be.

He recalled his own youth, the poverty in which he had lived, and his dreams of escaping it and being a great artist. He well remembered the fear and the pain that his impoverished existence had caused him in his childhood, and he could not stand to think that he had lost an opportunity to remove the same kind of fear and pain for another boy.

And worse, that boy's parents had died; he could not believe that he had turned his back on the child. Filled with shame and regret, and wondering what would become of the boy, wearily he made his way back home.

It was dark when he arrived back at his little cottage. The air outside has grown colder as the sun sank into the night. Stepping inside, he stamped the snow off his boots, and found his way to the hearth. Kneeling there in the dark, preparing a fire, he felt that familiar prickling up the back of his neck as the hairs stood on end.

'Oh, no!' he thought. 'How much worse can it get? What else can she do to me?!' Beaten and defeated, he was unprepared to do battle with the old crone. Though he had learned many valuable lessons, he did not believe that it would matter to her at all. She would exact her revenge; of that, he was certain.

He worked quickly and quietly, until he had finished lighting the fire. He was grateful for its warmth, as he sat, rubbing his hands together in front of it, all the while, knowing the crone was standing directly behind him. Without turning around, he finally said, with some exasperation, "What is it you want from me now? You've taken everything I had. I have nothing else to give; there is nothing else you can take away. What can you possibly want?"

There was a brief silence, followed by the now familiar sound of the rustling cloak, which filled him with dread and caused a shiver to race up his spine.

"Well? What is it, you old hag? The only thing you can take from me now is my life, and that's certainly not worth much after the things I've done. What do you want from me?"

"You," was the quiet reply.

His blood ran cold as he prepared to die. Terrified to turn around, his heart pounded so hard, he could feel it throbbing in his ears. The cloak rustled as she drew nearer. Aware that she was immediately behind him, the man nearly fainted as he felt her fingers clasp his shoulder.

"What are you going to do to me?" his asked, eyes wide with terror as he spun around to face his killer.

There stood his beautiful wife in a long, black cloak. Her hair, so dark and long, hung softly framing her delicate face and smooth, white skin.

"What -- what --" was all that came out of his mouth, as he faced her. She smiled, delighted by his confusion and the surprise.

"How did you find me?" he asked, obviously not comprehending what was happening.

"I've always known where you are. I have found you before."

"What do you mean? It was I who found you when we met. How do you always know where I am? I do not understand," he said, a look of bewilderment on his face.

"I mean, here, years ago, that night, and not long ago, at the castle..." She waited for him to figure it out. But he did not.

"The Transformation Potion, darling," she said, in a matter-of-fact way.

His eyes grew wide and he was at once astonished and horrified. "You!" he cried. "You are the crone?"

His lovely young wife smiled again, nodding as finally he understood.

"No! It cannot be! How...how can you..."

Again, she said simply, "The Transformation Potion, darling." And as she watched her husband recoil, she began to laugh.

The artist was faint from the shock, from the surprise, and had to sit, while his wife began to explain. "I was sent to teach you many lessons. Do you remember the promise that I made to you?"

"Yes," replied the artist, "of course I do. You promised to give me all I deserved, and you did, every step of the way. Although the lessons have been harsh, I needed them."

"You are right," said his beautiful young bride, "you did, and you have learned them well. You have learned that what is important in life is not what we can get, but what we can give. You have learned to have compassion, respect for yourself and others, and you have learned responsibility. You have learned that you cannot run from your fears; they will follow you everywhere, and will destroy you, if you so allow it.

"You have understood that even if you had created a beautiful painting to sell, you forgot who your customers would be, and you treated everyone with rudeness, disrespect and arrogance. But through your suffering, you have mastered many lessons, not the least of which is something else right here in this room."

The artist was further confused. To what could she be referring?

He looked around the room, searching for a clue to his wife's puzzle.

"The answer is in your paintings, my love," she continued. "Just look around you, and see what you have created."

The artist's eyes scanned the room, glancing from one painting to the next. Each one seemed to reach back out to him and speak to him, an echo of something deep in his soul. He thought he was beginning to understand.

"As a child, you lived in poverty. You were consumed by it, terrified by it, and could not see all the riches of having two parents who loved and supported you and your dreams, and who did their best for you. For years, your paintings were created out of your fear and your desire for money, which you thought would bring you happiness and peace.

"You had everything you needed, but all you saw was what you wanted and did not have, and your paintings told only stories of fear, and of greed and selfishness. They did not speak of love, or respect, gratitude or passion for anything except money. It was impossible for you to create anything desirable because of what was in your heart.

"But look around you, my love. These paintings speak volumes about all that is of value. There is compassion in these creations, there is humility, there is a soul, living and breathing in every one of them. You are no longer concerned with making a fortune with your gift; now you wish to paint purely for the love of it, for the love of expressing what is in your heart. Now you understand what it is to be a truly great artist."

The man stood in silence, absorbing all that his wife had told him. Finally, he realised what it was that had been different the night before, as he had been creating all these paintings. All the pieces of the puzzle were falling into place, and it was beginning to make sense to him.

With so much to overwhelm the artist, it had taken this long, but all of a sudden, another question rushed into his mind. "What about the crone? And you? I do not understand! How can you be one and the same? Are you really that horrible old woman?" he recoiled.

His wife chuckled and replied, "As I told you, I was sent to teach you many lessons. My appearance has always reflected what was in your heart. When you were a selfish boy, I came to you in your dreams, and then here and at the castle, reflecting the ugliness of what you held inside."

The artist felt somewhat embarrassed and ashamed by her statements, but he could not deny their truth.

"Do you remember the day we met?" she asked.

"Oh, but of course!" he replied.

"Think back," she said, "and remember what was happening immediately before you saw me on the cliffs."

The man closed his eyes, recalling that day as he stood on the balcony, delighting in the beauty of the ocean, the sun, feeling a sense of appreciation and peace that he had not known before. It was then that he had spotted her on the beach.

He did not need to say a word as he recalled these thoughts and feelings, because his wife spoke again. "Yes, you do remember. That little bit of appreciation for what was around you, for the gifts of the Universe; that was what prompted me to appear to you in the form in which you saw me on that day. And when you had returned to ugliness, I came to you once more as the crone."

He needed no further explanation, and he had to agree with her entirely. Everything inside him had been unbearably ugly, except for a little while after he had met and married her. He recalled his slide from that lovely place, and was horrified when her comment about her last visit as the crone jogged his memory about the child that he had abandoned.

"The boy!" he cried suddenly, "What about the boy that you wanted me to help? What will become of him? What can I do to help him? I no longer have anything to offer, but I so wish that I could turn back the clock and help him on his way!"

"I know you do, my darling, but it has already been done. You have already done everything he needed."

Once again, the artist was confused. "But I have done nothing! Nothing but abandon the lad!" he said, shame and guilt washing over him as before.

His wife laughed, tossing her head back, the hood falling to her back. "You were the boy, my love."

Once again he was confused, and growing frustrated with the continual adding of pieces to the puzzle. Every time he thought he had it figured out, his wife threw something else in his path. "What could you possibly mean?" he asked of her. "You said this was a boy whose parents had died, and he was destined to be a wonderful and gifted artist. My parents died when I was grown, and I have never been any kind of artist, only a man with a desire to paint!" he exclaimed.

"But you are wrong, my love. 'Tis true, you were, grown when your parents died. But you have always been that fearful little boy, huddling in doorways and freezing, living in poverty, screaming to get out of it. Even as an adult, you were still that hungry child who was destined to become a great artist. You had grown used to your monetary wealth, and had forgotten where you had begun. And when I came to you that night to make my request, your fear drove you to commit one of the worst possible crimes against the soul. You turned your back on yourself."

She let her words sink in, and saw her husband hang his head in shame, understanding more than he wanted to. After a moment, he looked up at her and asked, "With all of the terrible things I have done, how am I destined to become a great artist?"

Waving her hand around the room, she gestured toward the paintings, she waited for his eyes to follow. Her husband's brow still carried the furrows of a puzzled man.

"I still do not understand," he said quietly, looking from his paintings back to his wife. "A great artist? But how? I have turned so many away from me, and cannot imagine that anyone would ever buy a painting from me again, no matter how beautiful they might be."

Once again, the artist's wife laughed, and she replied, "First of all, you will find that there is much forgiveness in the world. There are many who will give you another chance when they see that all that you have learned. And secondly, much of the damage that was caused by your selfishness will be undone, reversed."

The man thought back to the kind young widow, whose husband and daughter were dead because of his actions. Surely, that could not be undone. He began to speak, but as in the past, his wife seemed to reading his mind. "Yes, you are right," she said, "Death cannot be reversed. But peace and happiness can be restored in many ways. And all the people who have suffered financial hardship and loss will find that the damage will be repaired before long."

And unbeknownst to the artist, as she spoke these words, the widow was finding baskets of food and new clothing in her cottage, the first of many such gifts that would help her along the way. And at the same moment, in countless other homes across the land, similar gifts were appearing, as magically, healing was beginning.

The man sank into a chair by the fire, overwhelmed by all that he had been told that evening. His wife followed, and sat in the one next to him.

Looking into her eyes, his own filled with tears. "I am so relieved to know the truth about the boy. I did not think I could live with myself, knowing that I had turned my back on a child that I could have helped, a child who needed my love and the stability of a safe home."

His wife smiled, and leaning forward, took his hands in hers. "You will have another chance, my love. There is another child who needs you."

The artist's eyebrows shot up, and he sat straight in his chair, eager for a chance to redeem himself. "Who? Who is it? What can I do? I have nothing, really, to offer, but please, tell me what to do! I will move heaven and earth to make a difference for this child!"

"I know you will," she replied, and taking his hands, she placed them on her belly, which he noticed was a little larger than when he had last seen his wife. He felt a tiny flutter under his hand, which startled him, causing him to pull away, and stare at his wife in surprise.

"Yes, my love," she said, smiling warmly at him. "We have created a child who needs his father, and you will be able to teach him all the things you have learned. You will, indeed, be a great artist, but it will be because you have a great understanding of what is really valuable in life. These are lessons you will pass on to our son, and to the other children who will follow."

The artist could not believe his ears! This had been the most magical evening of his life, the right kind of magic. He threw his arms around his wife, and kissed her passionately, as tears streamed down his face.

His heart overflowed with many emotions for which he could find no words. They welled up into his throat; he could not speak. All he could do was hold his beautiful wife in love, respect, and deep gratitude.

After a long embrace, the man pulled himself away. Blinking at his wife through his tears, he smiled the warmest smile he had ever felt on his face. But suddenly, a worrisome thought rolled through his mind.

"There is something troubling me," he said, an anxious tone in his voice. "You promised that I would get what I deserved. It is not right that things should turn out so beautifully for me. I have earned the position in which I have found myself, being back here, in this tiny cottage with nothing but the disdain of everyone who knows me."

Once again, his wife took his hands in hers, and looked deep into his eyes. "You are exactly right, my darling, you have earned the position in which you have found yourself. And that is the position of being a wonderful man, who has suffered and learned much, who has the love of an adoring wife, who will become a loving father, and who is already a great artist.

"Soon," she continued, "you will have the fame and fortune that you always desired, but it will come from an entirely different place, and you will always value and respect every bit of it. Your work is meant to help others in their own healing, and that will mean more to you than money ever did. You will get exactly what you deserve.

"I told you, I always keep my promises."

And they lived happily ever after.

LETHAL MEMORIES

My tortured soul cries, begs for peace, its voiceless screams unheard, tormented by events unseen, unremembered. Yet they stir and they rumble, spilling forth from deep within, the turmoil unmistakable. Silently, they poison, their stealth keeping them hidden from even the most dedicated seeker.

Thick and black, they invade and violate, leaving no blissful place untouched, unscathed, ensuring damage and destruction as they viciously tear through the most pure and innocent corners of the soul. Yet they remain unknown, unstoppable, mighty and growing, delighting in their deadly game.

And as they rip through my soul, hell-bent on annihilation, these hateful memories, locked away so deep inside, thrill at their power to destroy me, while remaining deathly silent, killing any joy, any peace, any tiny fragment of spirit they can find on their relentless mission.

Moments long past, long forgotten by Consciousness, yet recorded deep within the darkest places in my soul, diligently pursue their evil course, unwavering in their efforts to exterminate my spirit.

Almighty cowards that they are, their strength lies in their ability to permeate my soul invisibly, for I cannot do battle with an unseen enemy. A brave warrior would have no shame, would demand to be noticed, would give the hopeless opponent a chance to defend itself.

But not these Destroyers of my Soul, my Self. They lurk patiently, their tenacity unbeatable, taunting me with their bloody, savage game of "Hide and Seek But Never Find."

Intangible, secret, perfectly concealed, my constant and hidden companions, these vile memories lie in wait, viciously tearing at my soul, shredding wounds unhealed, forbidding, sabotaging any effort to find peace. I am powerless to stop them; they remain so well hidden.

Their silent, cancerous invasion seems somehow a contradiction to the vicious forcefulness with which they destroy me, a tiny piece at a time, sneering at me as they hear my false beliefs that I am strong and well, and able to heal, for they know better. They know there will be no healing. No, not really. And each time I utter words of strength, the power that I so foolishly believe I have gained is merely used to feed those long-forgotten moments in Time which ceaselessly work to destroy me, and they are entertained, their silent, jeering, maniacal laughter reverberating, echoing throughout my soul, haunting me for all eternity.

I AM DEVOURED

It waits. It creates the darkness as bait for tormented souls, whose obsession with it will entice. Then it lurks, silently, patiently, waiting to feed on its prey. I leave the light and enter its shadows. It is hiding there, still, as its ominous intentions creep forth, billowing and unstoppable.

I seem to have no will of my own. I am drawn to the shadows as I approach, my back to the light which grows dimmer with each of my hesitant steps, and fades imperceptibly, and now I am in blackness, though how it happened eludes me. It seems I must have always been surrounded by it; I no longer remember the light, which so quietly disappeared without my notice.

And in the blackness that it created, I know it is there, though I can't see it. I can almost hear it, a long, low rumbling, growling, or can I just feel it? Certainly, its presence is undeniable, unmistakable. To find oneself in its company is to become the prey, to know that survival is questionable. Doubtful. The predator is unrelenting, ceaseless in its desire for satisfaction.

I am captured. I am the hostage. I am bound. I am in chains. I cannot move. I am immobilized. And still it waits. It taunts and torments me; it teases me with glimpses of freedom in the light, and I think I may taste it again, as it relaxes its crushing grip. But freedom is mine no more. No, not even a taste, not a morsel. I am once again plunged into the darkness, where it delights in my terror, which amuses it so. It toys with me, contemplating whether to devour me, or to push me into the quicksand.

If its decision is to devour me, I wonder whether it will be with a gluttonous fervour, ripping and tearing, grunting in hedonistic pleasure as it tastes my blood, or whether it will be as a sensitive lover, teasing and tantalizing with strawberries, dangling each one just above full and slightly parted lips, the tongue delicately licking at them, darting in and out of the mouth, tasting the juices. And after a time, unhurriedly biting into the fruit, sensuously savouring each bit of its flesh, until the leisurely meal is swallowed in its entirety.

And if its decision is the push into the quicksand, it will take great pleasure in watching me struggle, it will delight in my desperation, and with every movement, I shall sink deeper still, until I am unable to move. The onslaught will be merciless as it violates and invades me, pushing its way past my nose, my mouth, my throat, forcing me to devour my own death.

I can do nothing but wait...wait in the black terror...wait to see whether my captor will release me...wait to see whether I am devoured, whether I will live or die...wait for the light, and wonder, hopelessly, if it will ever come...

THE STORY OF TRUST

Once upon a time, far, far away, in the Forest of Innocence, there lived a little girl named Trust. She was very small and delicate, and she lived with her Guardian, Love, in the Castle of Self-Esteem.

Trust was a very special girl, and when she was born, the Keeper of the Castle Gate created protectors for her. These soldiers were called Boundaries, and they were led by the strongest of them all, the Boundary of Self-Respect. Whenever Trust left the safety of the Castle, they followed her while she played in the Forest.

Being the Guardian of Trust, Love had an enormous responsibility, but she was joyful and honoured upon receiving the news that she had been given this duty. Each morning, she walked through the tall, forest trees, along a well-worn path to the clear, bubbling brook and carried its precious Waters of Self-Love back to the Castle to quench Trust's thirst.

The Spirit Within

Then Love would go into the Garden and pick a basketful of fresh Affirmations, upon which Trust would nibble throughout the day. Together, their lives were filled with peace and happiness.

One day, when the two of them were walking through the Forest, Love explained to Trust that when she was old enough, she would be given the Powers of the Magic of Life that would allow her to achieve anything her heart desired. As well, she would become Queen of the Forest of Innocence, and she would rule with a loving King at her side.

"For now," explained Love, "you have been given the power and responsibility to care for all the animals in the Forest. They are vulnerable and easily wounded or killed by forces Outside the Forest. But you have the power to keep them strong and safe. All you need to do is feed them from your hand every day and they will be well."

So from that day on, when Trust went to play in the Forest, she would gather nuts, leaves and berries, calling her animal friends to her as she made her way through the trees. Trust had always loved to play with the rabbits, squirrels, deer and other Forest creatures, and she was thrilled to learn that she was responsible for keeping them well and safe from harm. She loved her task, and happily filled her skirts with the foods that sustained her beloved friends. Yes, life in the Forest of Innocence was perfect.

There was, unbeknownst to Trust, a land Outside and not so far away. It was an evil land, ruled by a horrible man. He was King Violence and his Kingdom was the Land of Abuse. His home was the Castle of Self-Loathing, which was guarded by his soldiers, the Controllers. They were vicious, angry beasts that protected King Violence at all costs. They fed him Power constantly, for without it, King Violence would die. They brought him water from the swirling, black, boiling River of Hate. Over the centuries, it had pulled thousands of its victims into its angry depths, sucking the very life out of their lungs and replacing it with its vile waters. And with their torturous deaths, their Power was drained from their lifeless bodies, and into the angry waters providing strength for the evil King.

The Land of Abuse was the most terrifying place on earth, filled with poisonous snakes and lizards. There were deep Pits of Abandonment, great Fires of Rage, and dark Caves of Fear and Loneliness. In its Forests of Dead Black Trees, there roamed vicious Beasts of Destruction that devoured anything in their paths. The sun never dared go there, and the Wind howled constantly, its moans echoing hauntingly, ceaselessly throughout the Land.

The King possessed the Magic Powers of Transformation, which allowed him to make anything appear to be something it was not. But this was not enough for the greedy King. He wanted to possess the Powers of the Magic of Life, for they were far stronger than his own Power, and he envied everything they would bring. He knew they would belong to the Queen of the Forest of Innocence, so he devised a wicked plan the day he heard of the birth of Trust. Then he waited for the day when she would be old enough for him to act upon it.

As the years passed, he would often peer into his cracked mirror and let out a menacing, horrible laugh as he smiled his evil smile, thinking of his plan.

"Soon, Little One, soon," he would say to the mirror, as though he were speaking to Trust herself. "The day is almost upon us." And he would rub his rough, gnarled hands together in anticipation.

Meanwhile, in the Forest of Innocence, Trust was approaching the day of her Coronation. Though it was still quite some time away, there were many preparations to make. Soon she would be the

Queen of the Forest, and all her rightful Powers would be bestowed upon her. She had grown into a very beautiful young woman, graceful, delicate and sweet. As she grew, so, too, did the Forest. It became greener, thicker, more colourful and fragrant each day that Trust lived there. It was as if the Forest knew the great significance of the coming event and was decorating itself, preparing itself to be worthy of the New Queen's rule.

King Violence was also well aware that the day was rapidly approaching; he could hardly contain his excitement, for the time had come to begin putting his evil plan into action. One morning, he stood in front of the mirror, preparing to use his Powers of Transformation.

As he stared into the mirror, the sky grew much darker than its usual dismal grey, the thick, black clouds, rolling and boiling in the ominous skies. Jagged bolts of lightning tore through the sky, with deafening cracks of thunder. The Wind whipped through the Land, with a fierceness in its icy blast that made even the Beasts of Destruction quiver.

Suddenly, the Transformation took place. Gone was the hideous King Violence and in his stead, there stood a tall, handsome young man, with an air of dignity and royalty, and with strong, masculine features. There stood Prince Charming, dressed in the finest silk and linen, smiling to himself in the mirror as he admired his work.

Prince Charming prepared a proper coach and horses and began his journey to the Forest of Innocence. Once there, he paused for a moment outside its gates, readying himself for the task at hand. His fingers trembled with excitement as he slowly reached for the golden rings that would pull the gates open. They creaked and groaned, as it had been some time since they had been used. As they opened wide to Prince Charming, they might as well have been a mother's arms, welcoming and embracing a long-lost son.

Prince Charming's eyes grew wide when he saw the beauty of the Forest of Innocence. Hundreds of colourful butterflies floated silently through the air. The brilliance of the sunlight through the trees was almost blinding to the Prince's eyes; they were unused to its radiance. There was an explosion of colour in the thousands of unusual flowers, which burst forth from bushes, trees, the ground. Birds chirped and fluttered in the excitement of this honoured guest's arrival. The animals timidly poked their heads into the clearing, knowing something important was happening.

Nearby, under a gnarled old oak tree, Trust had just awakened from a nap in a soft bed of leaves and moss. She felt the excitement of her dear little friends and went to investigate. The energy in the Forest was dramatically different; it was almost vibrating and made Trust feel somewhat giddy. Her Boundaries felt it, too, and unsure of what it meant, they followed her closely.

Upon her arrival at the Forest entrance, Trust was met by a dashing young prince, who had eyes that looked deep into her soul, and a flashing smile that made her heart jump and beat faster than it ever had before. She felt light-headed, and had to sit on the root of a large tree to catch her breath.

Prince Charming was stunned by how beautiful Trust was; never had he seen anything like it. He could not wait to possess her. He knew the only way that would happen was to first gain the confidence of Love, and then he would destroy Trust's Boundaries. "And finally," he thought to himself, "the girl will be mine."

Almost immediately after the Prince entered the Forest, Love felt his presence. She hurried to the Gate, anxious to meet the long-awaited visitor. With one look into his beautiful, dark eyes, Love new Trust's Prince had come. The Boundaries always took their cues from Love, as she was responsible for Trust. As she appeared to be quite comfortable with this man, even though he had just barely arrived, the Boundaries relaxed their guard, and allowed him to venture nearer to Trust.

To ensure his true identity would not be discovered, with a small and unnoticed gesture of his hand, Prince Charming caused a fine mist to slowly begin to fill the Forest, so slowly that Love and Trust did not notice it was happening. But before too long, it was difficult for them to see anything clearly any more.

The Prince, Love, and Trust spent many hours together, talking, planning, sharing. The Boundaries were always close at hand, but as Trust felt increasingly safe with him, so did they, and they agreed to venture further away from their charge, at her insistence.

The Prince and Trust spent endless days holding hands, walking through the Forest, and Trust allowed the Boundaries to wander further and further away with the passage of time. Gently, the Prince would stroke Trust's hair or face with his fingers. Sometimes, she would carefully take his hands in hers, and kiss them ever so sweetly, expressing her deep love for him. She adored him, adored his loving hands, which caressed her so tenderly.

As Coronation Day drew nearer, Prince Charming knew it was time to move to the next phase of his plan to further ensure his secret would remain his own. He caused a rain to fall, and once again, using his Powers of Transformation, turned the raindrops into Lie-drops, so that the Brook of Self-Love was soon filled with lies, which Love unknowingly then gave Trust to drink every day.

As well, he transformed the Affirmations into Manipulation and Blame, but in the mist brought by the Prince, neither Love nor Trust noticed the difference. So when Love picked them from the bountiful garden and fed them to Trust, she was unwittingly doing the evil work of King Violence, participating in the destruction of

Trust, and ultimately, in the destruction of the Forest of Innocence. His deception caused Love to destroy everything she had worked so hard to nurture and build.

Each rainfall was harder than the last. The Lie-drops grew bigger, sometimes even so big as to cause damage to the flower petals, or the leaves of the Forest. Eventually, they had become so large as to injure the vulnerable little forest creatures. And finally, even Trust's delicate body was becoming increasingly covered with bruises.

Love began to hear Trust complain of feeling sick after eating the 'Affirmations', which neither of them knew had been transformed into Manipulation and Blame. The young girl grew steadily more ill each time Love fed her these destructive meals, yet neither had any idea what was happening.

During most of this time, Love remained loyal to the Prince, never guessing that he had any part in the strange goings-on in the Forest. But when she began to notice bruises and marks on Trust's body, and saw how weak and sick Trust had become, she began to suspect the Prince's involvement.

Love went to Trust with her fears, wondering if she felt the same way. But Trust was reluctant to discuss Love's concerns. However, in the few words she spoke, Love detected the first note of unhappiness ever uttered by Trust. It broke her heart to hear it. She felt that as a Guardian, she had failed Trust. As well, she was upset that Trust seemed to know something was wrong, yet she was choosing to ignore it. About this, Love could do nothing.

Prince Charming was quick to pick up on Love's change of heart. Suddenly, he was filled with fear, which threatened his plans. He became enraged and knew he had to act swiftly, before Love's suspicion grew or could be confirmed. He went to the garden to pick some Manipulation and fed it in large quantities to Love, Trust and the Boundaries. He followed it with a large pitcher of Lie-drops from the Brook. Then, when he had them all completely under his spell, the Boundaries fell asleep for the first time ever, leaving Trust completely open and vulnerable.

With that, he whisked her away to the Evil Land of Abuse and locked her in his Castle of Self-Loathing.

Once they were there, in that horrible, dark, terrifying place, Prince Charming stood in front of Trust and smiled. But for the first time, she saw that it was not the warm smile of the man she loved, but rather the satisfied, smug sneer of an evil, menacing stranger. As she stared at him, she was filled with terror, a feeling from which she had been protected her whole life. Never had she endured anything so threatening. She was frightened, isolated, trapped and utterly desperate.

As she stared into the Prince's face, it began to change, slowly twisting and contorting itself into the hideous face of the Evil King Violence. His eyes no longer looked at her with love, only with rage and possession. She shrank away from him as slowly, he moved toward her. She was out of her mind with terror. She had no Boundaries to protect her now, and the King's Controllers had silently stolen her Power and fed it to him on the way through the Gates. She was stripped of all her defenses.

What happened in that Castle of Self-Loathing was more than Trust could bear. The King violated her in a series of the most unspeakable ways imaginable. His hands, which had once touched her so gently and sweetly, now caused her unbelievable pain and humiliation at every level of her being. She felt utterly broken and destroyed.

Over and over again, for what seemed an eternity, the King

continued his reign of terror and violence. With each act of cruelty, a tiny part of Trust's heart would turn black, wither and die. By the time Trust was to have had her Coronation, there was but one small piece of her heart left. If that died, too, so would Trust.

Meanwhile, during Trust's imprisonment, the Forest of Innocence had been completely destroyed in a raging fire, which left Love horribly disfigured. With Trust gone, the Castle of Self-Esteem had crumbled. The Waters of Self-Love had disappeared, leaving the bed of the Brook dry and barren. Without Trust to feed them every day, the vulnerable Forest creatures had begun to die, one each day, until there was but one tiny little squirrel remaining alive, though seriously wounded by the Lie-drops.

The Boundaries were lost, roaming aimlessly, trying to remember who and what they were, except for their leader, the Boundary of Self-Respect, who was trying desperately to find Trust. His strength was failing, however, and he knew his time was limited.

Although Trust had not actually seen the Forest for some time, she could feel its changes in her heart. On what was to be her Coronation Day, Trust sat alone in her room and began to cry. She could not believe her life had turned into this hideous nightmare, or that Love had not been able to protect her, as she was meant to do.

As she sat at her dressing table, looking out across the dark, terrifying, desolate Land of Abuse, a teardrop rolled down her cheek and fell on her chest, directly above the one, tiny, remaining living part of her heart.

Suddenly, she felt something strange and warm in her chest. It was a feeling of Power, and a different kind of Power from any she had known before. She had not known that even without the ceremony of her Coronation, she was to be endowed with the Powers of the

Magic of Life on that day. So when this happened, she was somewhat afraid; she did not immediately understand what was happening. Soon, however, she recalled Love's words: "The Powers of the Magic of Life will allow you to achieve whatever your heart desires."

Realising this, she began to notice a feeling of strength she had not ever felt before, and she began to believe she could escape from this horrible Land. She closed her eyes, and silently called upon her Boundaries, praying they would hear. It was difficult at first; she couldn't concentrate. But she was persistent, and found that the more she tried, the easier it became.

Wandering in the Forest, the Boundary of Self-Respect was suddenly and powerfully struck by a vision of where Trust was. As he focused on the vision, he found himself being pulled in what he believed was the right direction. His steps quickened with excitement and a growing feeling of Power. He knew then that they had begun to reconnect.

As he rushed to help Trust, he happened upon the wounded squirrel, lying alongside the path. He carefully picked it up, and carried it with him, happy to be able to protect at least one tiny, vulnerable creature. Away the two of them went, in search of the other Boundaries, readying themselves to rescue Trust.

One by one, the Boundaries were found in various states of illness and injury after the turmoil and destruction in the Forest of Innocence. They had been wandering aimlessly, separately, powerless and unfocused. But once the group was assembled, they all noticed their strength began to grow and their focus quickly became clear.

Once they were together again, they gathered their strength. With clearer heads, it didn't take long for them to find the Evil Land of

Abuse. They had quite a battle with the Controllers at the Gate. King Violence was there to do his best to destroy them. He was furious that Trust had gained her Power and even more furious to discover that it was far greater than his own. More threatened than ever before, he stepped up his efforts to take it from her.

It was a vicious, savage battle. The Boundaries and the Controllers ripped and tore at each other. Swords and axes met flesh and bone. For a while, it was difficult to tell who would win. Suddenly, Trust's Powers turned the tide and the Controllers began losing limbs and heads until soon, they were all dead.

Then, using the Powers of the Magic of Life, with one final effort, she gave the Boundary of Self-Respect the strength he needed to plunge a sword into the King's black, withered heart. Instantly, the Howling Wind stopped. The Beasts of Destruction died. The River of Hate ceased its deathly churning and became still.

In the aftermath of the terrible battle, Trust, the Boundaries and the squirrel sat in the overwhelming silence, looking on with horror at the grisly scene before them. Everywhere they looked, there was death; a bloodied Beast, a Controller savagely torn to shreds. King Violence lay nearby, the sword that had pierced his heart, still in his chest, as if it were standing, a symbol of victory over the enemy.

As she sat in silence, absorbing the reality of the whole nightmare, Trust knew that she would never again be as she was before meeting Prince Charming. She sat quietly stroking the squirrel, and once again, began to cry. The wounded squirrel was even more vulnerable than when Trust had been given the responsibility for its care and safety, but her unwillingness to see the Truth had caused the deaths of all the Forest Creatures but this one.

She remembered the day Love tried to speak of her concern regarding Prince Charming, but Trust had refused to listen. She remembered, too, how she had allowed her Boundaries, her Protectors, to wander, leaving herself open to the Prince's destruction. She felt ashamed because of the part she had played in the unfolding of it all.

To remind herself of not only Prince Charming's actions, but of her own responsibility in the events, she named the squirrel 'Betrayal'. Ever so gently, she kissed the tiny, injured animal. He looked up at her with sad, brown eyes as she held him to her breast, weeping whilst she begged for forgiveness.

The squirrel looked knowingly into Trust's eyes, understanding all. Trust knew her actions would be forgiven, but not forgotten. Then magically, Betrayal disappeared from Trust's hands, and went to live in the black, withered part of her heart.

As soon as they all felt strong enough, Trust and her Boundaries began their journey back to the Forest of Innocence. When they arrived, Trust saw, for the first time, the destruction there. Falling to the ground, she wept bitterly, and was once again filled with great pain. The Forest of Innocence was no more. It was but a vast wasteland of smoldering ash, everything burned, black, dry, and dead. It was quite unrecognisable. It would be lost forever.

While absorbed in her memories, Trust was startled by a noise behind her. She turned, and gasped, horrified once again. There stood her once-beautiful Guardian, Love, her face and body dreadfully blistered, red and infected. She wanted desperately to pull Love close to her heart and hold her, but she was afraid it would cause her more pain. Love, too, wanted to embrace Trust, but her arms were so seriously injured, she did not want to risk spreading her infection to Trust.

The Boundaries looked on at this tragic, painful reunion. Everyone knew there was much healing to be done. And so, they all set out together, slowly walking hand in hand, journeying to the Land of Survivors.

When they arrived, they were welcomed at the Gate by several strong Boundaries. As they entered, they were most surprised to see that everyone there was terribly scarred, some more severely than others. But they all looked at Trust with the same knowing look with which Betrayal had gazed at her. She was stunned and relieved to learn that she and her dear friends were not alone in their pain, and that healing would happen here.

Soon they were all settled into comfortable rooms in the Castle of Self-Worth. With the Boundaries of so many wise victims to guard its Gates, and with the shared strength of their new friends, they knew that together, they would learn to live with their scars.

With the Forest of Innocence totally destroyed, Trust could never again delight in its beauty. She would lie awake at night and try to recall it in detail, but her memories were lost to her pain. It was only because of the Powers of the Magic of Life that she could get through each day, knowing that they were helping her to grow and heal. In her heart, there would always be Betrayal, but Trust knew that somehow, she would learn to carry on.

HOPE

Once upon a time, a lost and broken little girl wandered through the Black Forest in a cold and lonely land, where the sun never rose. Stumbling through the woods, she was frequently pierced and scratched by branches and thorns that she could not see. Occasionally, the dim light of the moon, barely visible through the thick trees overhead, would cast just enough light for her to make her way through the brush, as she tried to find her way home.

One night, the little girl thought she heard the quietest ripples of laughter and giggles, and soft strains of cheerful music. She wondered if it was just a vague memory that was trying to surface, like when you wake from a dream, and recalling it seems just beyond your grasp.

She listened harder, shivering in the cold, and tried to follow the sounds, as she made her way through the dark forest. The laughter and music grew louder as she stumbled along, praying that she had found a way out, a way home.

After wandering for quite some time, to a part of the forest where she had never dared venture before, suddenly she came upon a clearing, filled with sunbeams pouring in from the Heavens. Having spent so much time in darkness, it was a blessing to see the light, yet it was so bright, she squinted against it, shielding her eyes with her arms.

She stood quietly hidden amongst the trees, peering through the branches, and before long, her eyes grew wide with wonder, as she peeked into this place which was far from the depths of the Black Forest. There, in the clearing, was a quaint little village full of elves and pixies, playing games, dancing, chasing each other and giggling. Beautiful, cheerful music drifted through the sweet air, yet she could not determine its source. Everyone seemed to be having so much fun, and she longed to join in.

But she was lost and broken. They were not. They were elves and pixies. She was not. She hesitated, wondering whether she should make her presence known, when suddenly, one of the elves stopped his game of tag and stood straight and unmoving, as if he had heard a sound. Listening intently, he carefully began to search the surrounding trees with his eyes. Those around him also stopped what they were doing, as they noticed that he seemed to be searching for something.

Soon, he spotted the girl, hiding in the trees. "Look!" he cried, pointing in her direction. "There's another one!"

The little girl was frightened, not knowing what fate might befall her. She stood frozen, afraid to remain, but unable to run

Suddenly, all eyes were upon her. With mounting fear, her heart beat wildly in her chest. And just as suddenly, there were whoops and cheers, as everyone rushed toward her, laughing and calling to her as they ran.

Realising that she was being welcomed into their circle, her fear quickly dissolved into excitement, as this happy and playful little group leapt and squealed around her. Gingerly making her way through the last of the sharp branches, she stepped into the beautiful sunlight. Closing her eyes, she bathed in its radiant glow, delighting in its warmth after being so long in the cold Black Forest.

Over the following days, the elves and pixies tended to her wounds. They fed her, nourished her, coaxed and encouraged her to heal and to be well again. They taught her many things, and supported her constantly through her recovery.

Little angels appeared now and then, quietly inspiring the friends, letting them know how to help the little girl, and she was told that they were responsible for the music that played continuously. It was their constant reminder to this little group that each one was special and loved by a Higher Power.

At first, it was strange to be so readily welcomed into this happy little village, but soon it began to feel like Home. It did not take long for her to adjust to her new surroundings, to adopt their ways and make them her own. Although it was peculiar at first, she enjoyed their habit of feeding each other, rather than themselves.

Days were spent playing and laughing. And at night, before everyone settled in for a well-deserved rest, they gathered at the Brook of Wishes and Dreams and drank together. It was said that if they wished hard enough, their dreams would all come true.

Soon the little girl was thriving, happily laughing and playing with her new friends. She was certain that they had no idea what they had done for her, how many wounds they had healed, how much they had given her. She struggled to find the words to tell them "Thank you", to let them know what it meant to her to come from the cold, lonely Black Forest, and to be welcomed into this beautiful village with such wonderful friends, but the words never came. She only hoped that somehow, they would know what was in her heart.

One day, the little girl was playing with a couple of pixies near a pretty little pond. Giggling and chasing each other, they collapsed in laughter near its edge. The little girl had never seen such clear, sparkling water, and she leaned over the edge to see if she could see the bottom of the pond.

Astonished, the reflection looking back up at her was that of a pixie! She did not know what to make of this; was it a magical pond, where pixies dwelt? She knew that pixies can be mischievous, and wondered if her little friends were simply playing with her. But as she formed the words to ask them the question, she saw that the pixie in the water seemed to be saying the same words at the same time.

Puzzled and bewildered, the little girl shook her head, and looked again at the reflection, pointing at it, and telling her friends to take a look. In a moment, as she peered into the water, she saw her friends and the pixie staring back. Her friends giggled beside her, as she struggled to make sense of this.

The pixies explained that this place, far from anywhere, was a magical place, and that lost and broken children found healing there, and became elves and pixies. No longer was she lost or broken. No longer was she different from her friends. They were all the same.

Not long after this revelation, the new little pixie was sitting by the Brook of Wishes and Dreams, alone except for the flowers, and the little animals that would sometimes come and sit with her for a while. Although she loved to play with her friends, she enjoyed slipping away to spend some time daydreaming, too. It was fun to play "I wish, I dream", even though she knew those things would never come to pass.

She sprawled out on the cool, green grass in the shade of an old oak tree, and closed her eyes. Completely lost in her dreams, and having a wonderful time, a gentle little smile formed on her lips.

The new little pixie was so lost in thought that it took her a while to notice, through closed eyes, the bright glow that seemed to come from nowhere. From the depths of her daydreams, it finally occurred to her that lying in the shade, there should not be such a light.

Opening her eyes, she saw an Angel, standing there in front of her, surrounded by a radiant light. She was very different from the sweet little angels who had wandered in and out of the village, checking on things, seeing to everyone's needs; this Angel was very beautiful, and it was apparent that she was also very powerful.

The little pixie sat up and rubbed her eyes, wondering if she had fallen asleep and was dreaming, yet the Angel did not vanish. Instead, she spoke to the pixie, telling her that all her wishes and dreams were about to be fulfilled. "Everything that you were just imagining will come true," said the Angel. "You will see. It will all become real very soon. But it will mean you have to leave your friends here."

The pixie was stunned. Her dreams would be fulfilled? How could this be so? Why would it happen to her? And why would she have to leave her friends? Bewildered, she asked the Angel these questions, but the only reply that came was a kind smile before she drifted skyward, disappearing into the bright sunlight, as the little pixie stared after her.

Sitting alone and astonished for some time, the little pixie could not understand what had happened. She spent some time trying to decide if the visit from the Angel had simply been a dream, incredulous at the notion that all her wishes would be fulfilled, and deeply saddened that it meant leaving her beautiful friends, and this wonderful place.

The little pixie stretched out on the grass again, and stared up at the clouds as they floated gently across the sky, considering all that the Angel had said, and what she needed to do.

She struggled with the concept of leaving this place; it had been such a source of healing, support and laughter. She tried to imagine actually leaving, and saying goodbye, but then she remembered that they all sat together every night, drinking from the Brook of Wishes and Dreams, and she knew that just as she would encourage all of her friends to follow their dreams, they would do the same for her.

While the pixie lay in quiet contemplation of her future, unbeknownst to her the Angel made a very special appearance in the village, telling the pixie's friends what had happened, and asking them if they would like to do something wonderful for her.

The friends were overjoyed by the news of the pixie's incredible luck. Immediately, they set about the task of preparing a very special celebration for her, wanting to surprise her upon her return from her daydreams.

And surprise her, they did! As the sun was beginning to set, the little pixie wandered back into the village, lost in thought about the impending changes in her life, and was stunned by what she saw.

There, in the clearing, was the biggest celebration she had ever witnessed! An enormous banner was suspended from the arch of the gate with a congratulatory message for her. Vibrant streamers hung from trees and the cottages, and all the tables were covered with brightly coloured cloths, and a feast fit for a king. The entire village had been decorated with a stunning array of colours, shapes and patterns in a collection of beautiful works of art, which they had made themselves, and were dedicating to her.

She was so overwhelmed by these very loving gifts that she stood, motionless and unable to speak, eyes wide and filling with tears. After a few moments, her friends noticed her there, at the edge of the clearing, and instantly, there were cheers, as they rushed toward her, telling her that an Angel had told them her wonderful news, and had arranged this celebration of the occasion.

As they gathered excitedly around the little pixie with words of congratulations and well wishing, they said that they would miss her when she left. She was most surprised when many of her friends spoke of their sadness at her leaving, or of how much she had meant to them; she really did not expect to hear such kind words from most of the ones who shared their feelings. Some of them had written beautiful messages and poems for her, which they read to her at the party that evening.

The little pixie was so overwhelmed by such an outpouring of support, friendship and love that she could only weep as her heart overflowed with appreciation for all that her friends and the Angel had done for her.

During the celebration, the little pixie sat in a place of honour, which had also been beautifully decorated with her friends' creations. Her eyes wandered from table to table, each filled with the joyful faces of her friends, laughing and chatting amongst themselves over their feast, candles flickering in the evening breeze. She marvelled at the wonderful works of art that her friends had created, and the words they had written just for her. She contemplated the wishes and dreams that were about to be fulfilled, and could not believe that all of these incredible things could be happening to her.

But as wonderful as all the dreams would be when they came true, it was going to be very hard to leave this beautiful place. And once again, as she sat quietly, trying to drink it all in, she was so overcome with emotion that her eyes filled with tears. At that moment, the biggest, most powerful wish she had ever had rose up in her heart. She wished so hard that her wonderful friends and the Angel could see all that she felt about them, what they meant to her, and what they had done for her.

Just then, the Angel drifted downward from the Heavens, lighting up the evening sky as if it were mid-day. All the chatter stopped, as everyone looked up, watching as she floated silently until she was standing in front of the little pixie, arms outstretched. The pixie rose and the Angel embraced her. Then holding the pixie away from her, she spoke so that all could hear.

"As you all know, your friend has wishes and dreams that are about to be fulfilled. But at this moment, she has one that is even more important than all the others."

She turned the pixie so that she was facing the crowd, the Angel standing behind her with her graceful hands on the tiny shoulders.

And suddenly, the little pixie's chest began to glow. The light grew brighter and stronger, and all eyes were fixed upon it as it began to reach out, like little sunbeams that went directly from her heart to each of the hearts of her friends, and to the heart of the Angel.

When the light extended from the pixie to everyone else present, they all gasped as they found themselves feeling as though they were right inside her heart! Each one could feel her deep gratitude, appreciation and love for her friends and for the Angel, and what they had done for her. It was a very magical moment for all present; no one had ever witnessed anything like it before.

Tears fell from many eyes as everyone felt connected like never before. The light began to fade as the little pixie threw her arms around the Angel in a heartfelt embrace, trying to find words of gratitude, but she could find none that seemed adequate. The Angel simply smiled, and said that she already knew all that was unspoken.

The Angel turned to the little pixie, and looking solemnly into her tiny face, she said, "Now, my dear, you must say your goodbyes. It is time."

The pixie turned back to her friends, and everyone shared their final hugs and a few quiet words. With the last goodbye, the Angel gathered the little pixie up in her arms and silently began to drift into the night sky, her radiant glow lighting their way.

Below them, all eyes watched, and all hands waved, until the light faded and the Angel could be seen no more. They were silent for a while, still looking Heavenward, trying to absorb all that had happened on this very magical day. Although they missed their little friend, they were happy to know that she was traveling to the Land of Wishes and Dreams. And as they quietly headed toward the Brook for their evening drink, they had renewed hope that one day, they would join her.

THE SPIRIT WITHIN

The Keeper of the Stars was very busy. Indeed, there was always much to be done, as he tended these Mirrors of our Souls. It seemed that no sooner had he finished his duties with one Spirit, there was another coming to see him with Approval Documents and the accompanying Certificate Verifying Past Lives, watching as he put on his spectacles, and peered at the papers through wise, grey eyes. Having determined that the paperwork was in order, he would set about the task of carefully selecting a perfect, pure crystal star, which was befitting the Spirit as it began its chosen New Life.

There were times when the Keeper of the Stars could not help but smile to himself as he read the documents and saw what a Spirit had chosen for the Next Life, and Lessons to be Learned. Sometimes, the Spirits saw him gently shaking his head from side to side, his long white hair and beard moving back and forth, like quiet little ripples on a summer pond. The younger ones had not yet learned to be unconcerned with the opinions of others. Often, they wondered just what the Old Man was thinking, but they were careful not to ask the question, for they knew he would only frown in response, silently telling them that they ought to know better.

The Spirit Within

The older ones paid no attention to what he may have thought of their choices, for they knew it mattered not at all. The Lessons were still required, whatever anyone's feelings about them might have been. The previous Lessons had taken immeasurable time and study; the preparation would not be wasted. All of them knew what needed to be done, when it was time, and when they were ready to carry on.

As that time drew nearer, the Spirits would often become restless, having taken as much time as was needed to absorb all the knowledge and information gained through previous Lives, and preparing for the challenges and Lessons in the next. With the new challenges identified, it was time to select a Life that would allow the best possible opportunities to face them, and to learn their Lessons.

And so it was that one day, a little Spirit stood before God and Goddess, Creators and Parents of All Spirits, seeking approval for the New Life it had chosen. As a part of Lessons learned in Previous Lives, this Spirit, although very old, had regained much of its youthful and childlike quality.

This was always pleasing to God and Goddess, for they knew it meant a Spirit was nearing completion of the Wheel of Learning. They smiled warmly when this sweet and gentle Spirit began to speak, for they heard an intriguing combination of Wise Old Soul, and Child Filled With Wonder, the best of all between the Beginning and the End.

They were not surprised when this Spirit requested a Life which would be fraught with great loss, much pain, and many difficult lessons, for they knew it was the next step required in the Progression of the Learning. Because they knew what was about to unfold, God and Goddess could not help but feel conflicted; they were protective of this Child of Theirs. As any parents, watching children grow and take steps which are necessary but which will cause pain, God and Goddess felt some ambivalence, knowing of the heartache that this Child was about to endure, and wishing they could prevent the inevitable hurting.

However, as with many aspects of parenting, they knew it was entirely necessary to let go. It was meant to be exactly as it was going to unfold, and therein lay the deep respect and honour that came with knowing absolutely that it was well within the Child's ability to handle the Life it has chosen. Already, they were eagerly anticipating watching the Child enjoy new learning and many new experiences.

God and Goddess knew they would be patiently waiting for the Lessons to be learned, ready to be there to offer guidance and comfort when the harsh, cold Winds of Life would howl, as they slammed the Child Spirit into the rocks and stormy seas of Lessons needing to be learned. They looked forward to the day that their Child would return Home from the next Life, ready to receive the honours that would be due after much achievement and accomplishment.

The radiant little Spirit, eyes wide and bright, approached God and Goddess, who were seated on their thrones. They smiled warmly at this Spirit, standing there before them, and welcomed all who were present. The Angel in Charge of Proceedings sat behind his desk, shuffling papers and dipping a beautiful, feathery quill into an ink pot as he began to prepare the necessary documents.

When everyone was ready to begin, Goddess spoke, her voice low and soothing. "You stand before us today, believing you have completed your current Study and Lessons, ready to choose your Next Life and continue on your Journey of Learning. We have been watching your progress since the Beginning of Time, and we are most pleased with all you have learned."

Spirit was beaming, delighted with such an acknowledgement.

Goddess continued. "You have had many Lives, and have become very wise through your mistakes, your experience and your diligent studies. Of course, your Lessons grow more difficult with each New Life, as you become increasingly capable of handling such challenges. Tell us, please, about the New Life and the Lessons you have chosen, beginning with the foundation for them, which you so carefully laid in your Past Lives."

Spirit needed no encouragement to begin, clearly outlining Past Life experience and learning, as well as the chosen New Life, and Lessons that it was hoped would be mastered. It was most certainly going to be a long and arduous journey, but Spirit was not afraid. Rather, the telling of the Life and the expected Lessons was delivered with much conviction and enthusiasm, and with a strength that seemed contradictory to the gentle sweetness of this childlike Spirit.

Occasionally, God and Goddess smiled knowingly at each other, nodding gently, confirming their understanding of, and agreement with all that they heard. It was not their habit to interrupt or to ask questions during these orations; it was essential that each Spirit be allowed to speak until there were no more words, so that God and Goddess could make a proper assessment, based purely on what had come from a Spirit's own pondering and learning, and not altered by any hint or suggestion that they may have given.

At the conclusion of the lengthy disquisition, the little Spirit drew in a long breath, and letting it out slowly, stood quietly, waiting. God and Goddess had been most impressed by what they had heard, and needed no time between them to grant their approval.

"Once again, you have been diligent in your studies, and have proven yourself to be well-prepared for the challenges which you have so eloquently described," said the Goddess.

"Indeed," added God. "We have no doubt that you will succeed in this Life, and in these Lessons, and that you will return Home to us with an even deeper understanding of The Greater Plan. We will be watching you, Child. You will not be alone on your Journey. Go now, with our blessing."

The little Spirit ran to her Parents and the three shared a warm embrace, knowing it would be their last for a very long time.

The Angel in Charge of Proceedings had been listening intently to this shy little Spirit, and felt a tugging at his heart when he heard the lengthy list of Lessons that were to be tackled in the New Life. He looked somewhat dubious, despite the fact that he had witnessed countless such appeals since The Beginning of Time, and despite the fact that this particular Spirit truly seemed to have got all the homework done, and was as prepared as any he had ever seen. The previous Lessons all fit, the analysis was thorough and the delivery was exceptional.

But the uneasiness within him grew. He did not often get too involved with the Spirits when they made these applications, but something about this one was different. He supposed it was the quiet, childlike manner of this Spirit, which made him question whether the New Life was going to be overwhelming. He feared that on some other day, it would be too much for this gentle little Soul who stood before God and Goddess.

His heart skipped a beat when approval was given, and he was asked to fill out the necessary documents. His doubtful expression quietly changed to one of concern, which he tried to cover with a nervous smile, as the Spirit left the embrace and hurried to his desk to collect the papers. Hiding his feelings, he handed the completed paperwork to the excited little Spirit, who thanked him and skipped off to see the Keeper of the Stars.

When he was certain he would not be overheard, the Angel approached the God and Goddess. "Begging your pardon, I know I have no right to question your judgement, but with all due respect, I must speak. Did you not see the many places along that path that this Spirit was in danger of returning too soon? There were too many breaking points. There are many places in which that Life is as delicate as a porcelain plate. A tiny tap in just a certain way, at a certain moment, and it will shatter."

Both God and Goddess listened carefully to the Angel's concerns, then Goddess gathered her silver gown about her, and rose from her throne of moss, leaves and flowers. Smiling as she approached the Angel, she stretched out her hands to take his, seeing his fear and worry, and wanting only to reassure him

"You will see," she said, with the utmost confidence, as she looked directly into his eyes. "There are many potential breaking points in that Life, yes. But this Spirit has strength and a will that will fortify and protect it from all of that. Do not be fooled by such a childlike appearance; there is great strength and wisdom in that Spirit. I agree; it does seem a lot for one Life. And there will, indeed, be many times when Spirit is balancing rather precariously along potentially lethal cliffs. But I believe that it will be purposeful. This Spirit will overcome those rocks and storms, and will surprise many. You will see. You must trust."

"But Goddess," the Angel replied, "We know that sometimes the Lives are not completed in the way everyone hoped, or the way the Spirit planned. You know that it is always risky when Spirits choose the Lesson of Finding Strength Versus Giving Up. It is one of the hardest Lessons, and the Spirits do not always master it, as they thought they would. Sometimes, that Lesson overwhelms the

Spirits, and they choose to come Home before it is time. They do not realize that they will merely have to repeat the Lesson; it is such a waste, so much suffering for nothing."

Goddess took one of the Angel's hands in both of hers and held it tightly. "You know it is never 'for nothing'," she reminded him. "We know that some things are Meant To Be. And we know the Spirits have Free Will. They all make the best choices they can, based on the circumstances in which they have put themselves, whether it is in the choosing of their New Lives, or in the living of them. We must trust that it will all turn out for the best, which humans commonly think means that things will turn out the way they want them to do.

"You know that all conditions of The Lives serve a Higher Purpose; they are all part of the Greater Plan. The Lessons must be taught in the best possible way for each Spirit to learn. You must trust that everything that happens is for the highest possible good, no matter how it may look on the surface."

She was right; he did know these things, and he knew them well. Yet this time, something felt different. The Angel's fears were not at all relieved. The Goddess could not reassure him that the little Spirit would be all right in the New Life; she could only tell him that he must accept whatever happened as being the best possible outcome. His anxiety only grew as he watched the Spirit skipping off into the distance, paperwork in hand, the wheels now set in motion for what the Angel believed would be an ominous chain of events.

The little Spirit needed no reminders to find the Keeper of the Stars, having had countless Lives before this one, and knowing well how to find the Old Man. He heard the little footsteps approaching, and turned to greet the excited Spirit. "Ah, welcome!" he exclaimed. "How delightful to see you once again!

It has been a very long time; you must have been studying rather earnestly since your last Life."

"Yes, indeed, Sir," was the serious reply, as Spirit handed the papers to him.

"Please, do sit down," he offered, gesturing toward a chair. "Let me see now..." he said, as he squinted and peered through his spectacles at the first page. As he read, he sank into a very large old chair and immediately, it was apparent that all his concentration was directed to the contents of the documents.

Spirit sat obediently, and waited as he read every word very carefully. His was not an easy task. He had to consider all that had been learned in Previous Lives, along with what was expected in the New Life, and decide how large the crystal star must be in order for it to fulfill its role.

Spirit watched his face as he read all the relevant information, his eyebrows occasionally rising together, as if in surprise, or one at a time, as if in concern. Occasionally, he stroked his long beard thoughtfully as he read, and finally, he put down the pile of papers, laid his spectacles on top of them, and looked at the little Spirit, sitting so quietly and patiently in front of him.

With a warm and loving look, he said, "I know just the perfect crystal for you. I have been watching you since The Beginning of Time, and have been waiting for the day when it would mirror your essence. Come along; let me show you!"

With that, the Old Man guided Spirit through the Heavens, and as he did so, Spirit wondered about the star that he had chosen to reflect the continuing journey of such an Old Soul.

After drifting through the Heavens together, the two arrived at an immense, flawless and incredibly brilliant crystal star. It was so beautiful, in fact, the humble Spirit could only weep, for there were no words to describe such perfection.

"This? This is the star you have chosen for me?" Spirit cried, eyes wide with surprise and delight.

The Old Man smiled. "You have come a long way. You are deserving of this. Anything less exquisite would be unable to fulfill its purpose."

Gazing upon the flawless crystal, Spirit's face fell with sobering thoughts of its purpose, of What Was To Come. After a few quiet moments, Spirit turned to the Old Man and hugged him like a child embracing a father. Holding each other for a moment, they said farewell.

The Old Man stood back, hands on Spirit's shoulders, a wise and knowing look on his kind and lovely face, those beautiful grey eyes, watching and waiting for the moment Spirit would be ready for the next step.

And finally, it came. Spirit drifted toward the crystal, pausing immediately in front of it just long enough to turn and give a loving look of respect and appreciation to the Old Man.

On turning back to face the star, the Spirit suddenly began to glow, becoming a bright, radiant energy, engulfing the star, swirling faster and faster, and passing right through it, charging it with Spirit's energy, the crystal becoming so brilliant, it was difficult for the Keeper of the Stars to keep his gaze upon it.

Suddenly, after one explosive flash, Spirit vanished, having gone to inhabit the tiny being that would manifest it on the physical plane. The crystal star, suspended in its place in the dark skies, had finally begun to fulfill its purpose.

The Old Man could only wait for the day, some long years down the road, when its role would be completed, and it would illuminate the Heavens.

And so began Spirit's New Human Life as a girl and immediately, she was very aware of feeling unloved and unwanted. 'Ah,' she thought to herself, 'I remember choosing this Lesson'. How tragic that she was merely one new cell, supposedly safe inside her mother's womb, and already, she felt lost and threatened, knowing that she had chosen parents who were young and unable to care for her, and who would contemplate tearing this tiny scrap of life from the mother's body, thus immediately filling the little Spirit with fear for her very survival.

The seeds of self-destruction were sewn. It would be a powerful imprinting of the belief system that went to the core of the child: she had no value, nor did she deserve to exist. The battle had begun: her instinctive will to live versus her belief that she should die. It was a battle that would not soon end.

All of this happened in a flash, as Spirit entered the single cell that would one day become a little girl who lived in a frightening, hostile environment. The Lessons had begun. And in the same moment, far away in the silent sky, a tiny piece of the beautiful crystal shattered.

The Keeper of the Stars was still standing next to it, Spirit having vanished just an instant before, and upon witnessing this heartbreaking sight, a heavy tear rolled quietly down his soft cheek.

With each passing day, as with every Life before, the memories of the Spirit World and the reasons why she had chosen this Life were fading, and Spirit realized that her humanness was taking over, as it needed to do. She likened it to falling asleep, albeit for a rather long time in some Lives.

But even in sleep, one is still somewhat aware of one's surroundings. Spirit would still be present, but overshadowed by the Human element, which had to be strong in order to allow Spirit to have the Human experience. This would ultimately lead her to the required learning, if she managed to stay on her chosen path. Eventually, the Spirit would awaken, and then...well, then things would be different.

Before long, while still a tiny Human, all conscious memory of Spirit Life disappeared, and the little girl was left to begin her difficult journey, feeling all alone and frightened.

The Keeper of the Stars knew very well what was happening to the little girl. As the Old Man wandered through the Heavens, tending to the needs of the stars, occasionally he would pass her beautiful crystal 'mirror' and see the steadily worsening damage.

Having read her Application, it did not surprise him, but it was no less heartbreaking to witness. He understood how it all worked; he knew about the Lessons and the Greater Plan, and what was Meant To Be. But that never made it easier to know the Spirits were being hurt when he saw the cuts, chips and cracks in the precious crystal stars as they hung quietly in the dark sky, waiting.

The time came for the girl to enter the world as a separate little person, setting out on the journey that was her new Life. The Human parents who had provided the body for this little Spirit were very young, barely more than children themselves, and therefore, were unable to give the child the kind of love that would have allowed her to thrive.

Their own journeys had been exceptionally painful and difficult as well, and although it was not their intention, the little girl had been brought into an environment that was cold, lonely and hostile. She was already imprinted with the belief that she was unloved, unwanted, unimportant. Already, she had learned that to be loved meant she was helpless and powerless. Already, she had learned that the people who were meant to love and care for her were people who made her fear for her safety, themes that would be re-created again and again in this Life.

And so she was set on a course of trying to learn the truth about Perfect Love, Perfect Trust, and Perfect Acceptance. But it would be many long and painful years until those Truths were shown to her.

The young parents had their own challenges and Lessons to learn, and theirs were, of course, connected to those of the little girl. They had been chosen for many reasons, reasons that the Spirit knew when she was preparing for this Life, but which were unbeknownst to the child. Their role had been to provide an Earthly form for the Spirit, and to lay the groundwork for the Lessons that she was required to learn.

But these people were not destined to see the girl through to adulthood. The Parents, young and frightened, were ill equipped for parenting, though they did their best with the task during the time that they had been given to try.

In time, the Father's Lessons took him to a terrible place, the kind that the Human experience does not understand, but it was of the kind that God, Goddess and the Spirits knew were Meant To Be. And in that terrible place, the father killed his wife, and then himself, his young children watching in horror, their innocence violently torn from them in that moment.

Separated from all original family and siblings, the little girl had been placed with her Earthly Parents. In this Earthly Family, she found confirmation that love means violation, judgement, rejection and betrayal, especially from the Mother. She was destined to be the best teacher for the girl, compounding every lesson even once the little girl became a woman. It was the perfect situation; the girl was subjected to the soul-murdering behaviour of this very young Spirit.

The seeds of the Lessons had long since been sewn. In toxic soil, they had taken root and would continue to grow. Although the girl was unaware of Spirit moving inside her, it was there, urging her to carry on, in the hopes that someday, the Lessons that were to come from this situation would be learned, and true healing would finally begin. But until that time, the Old Man would frequently hear the soft tinkling of glass breaking, as piece by piece, the crystal would be almost completely shattered.

The girl endured unending abuse from the Mother, ceaseless insults and shaming words. The harsh and unnecessary judgements and criticisms were relentless, and once they had taken a firm hold in the little girl's mind, and in her Soul, the Mother did not even need to say them any more. The girl had absorbed the Mother's beliefs into every cell, and once those beliefs were integrated into her Soul, it was exceptionally difficult to begin to undo the damage, to change the beliefs, and to heal the terrible scars. This undoing was going to be one of the Spirit's hardest Lessons. But she had chosen this Mother for that very reason.

There were countless attacks against the girl by the Mother, whose cruelty caused her no end of pain. The Mother went so far as to violate the girl in a sexual way until the child was about twelve years old, and with vicious words, insulted and humiliated her on a regular basis. Home and family should have been safe and comforting. But for the girl, there was only fear and shame.

The Father, the only one who was at all loving and gentle with the girl at times, had experienced his own painful journey. It had led him to escape into a blur of alcoholism, his sensitive soul unable to cope with the harsh realities and crushing disappointments of life. His own wounds left him unable to see or to prevent the physical and intimate assaults on his daughter. He was not meant to master the Lessons that would have enabled him to change the situation. Those Lessons would have to wait for another Life, in order for the girl to learn hers in this one. All of this was part of The Greater Plan; all of it was Meant To Be.

Despite the physical, sexual and emotional violence in her family, and the constant fear she felt, the girl trusted her parents to do what was best for her. She needed to believe that they loved her. From the beginning of her physical existence in this Life, she had learned that love meant fear; it was as simple as that.

The girl grew into a woman, and the trusting continued, not just with the Mother, but with many other people. From childhood, she learned that she was expected to give up her power and control to anyone who wanted them, or she would risk more danger. Therefore, she kept connecting herself with people who validated those beliefs, reinforcing the learning that love meant painfully giving up the Self.

These relationships did not begin this way, however; at least, not on the surface. In the early days, it was always the same... words of flattery, words of need, words of love. Many of these men seemed to know just what the woman needed to hear. So easily, they spoke those words, with as much passion and conviction as it took to make her believe them. And because of her desperate need to be loved and wanted, she did.

Once she was hooked, the abuse and rejection began, always slowly and quietly at first, but just enough to play on her fear of being abandoned and unloved, which ran through to her very soul. In response to this fear, she would try harder to please, to be loved, and so the cycle would continue, eventually becoming a downward spiral, spinning out of control, seemingly unending. The more abuse and rejection she endured, the more she felt she deserved it, the more she tried to be worthy of being loved. It was eating her alive.

The woman's unhealthy relationships extended beyond the men with whom she became involved; she found the same themes repeated in every area of her Life. Often, with her friendships, she found that she was so desperately searching for love, that she was willing to give up her Self to find it.

With such a toxic foundation at the core of all of so many of her relationships, she was doomed to be miserable. And there were times that because of her own pain, or the poor choices she made because of it, she was the cause of suffering in others, including her own children, thus perpetuating a vicious cycle of hurt.

Time and time again, she was puzzled, even bewildered by the fact that no matter what she did, she could not find peaceful and loving relationships. She struggled to understand why it would always go wrong, why love always meant fear and repeated attempts to break her Spirit. She was always fighting to make things better, although her attempts were futile.

She knew something was wrong, she knew something was missing, but the knowledge of it was always just beyond her grasp. Although she was unaware, her desire to understand meant Spirit was moving inside her, urging her to continue her search for Perfect Love, Perfect Trust, and Perfect Acceptance.

There were times the woman was nearly beaten, so close to defeat that she would almost prove the Angel right, choosing to give up, rather than learn the Lesson of Finding True Strength. But something always pulled her back from the edge. It took her many years to understand what that 'something' was, and it did not come all at once. The countless painful bits and pieces of the woman's Life had to be put together like a long and miserable puzzle before Spirit was finally allowed to peek through and illuminate the dismal human existence that had been chosen so long ago for the Higher Purpose.

It was then, when Spirit finally reached out and connected with the woman, that the healing was about to begin.

Of course, the woman had always been unaware of Spirit's presence in her life, moving quietly, sustaining her, feeding her, even when she thought she would break. It was Spirit, who had been the source of the woman's strength, allowing her to endure her long and difficult struggles. Without it, they would have completely destroyed her, thereby making the Angel's words prophecy rather than simple concern.

But then came the turning point. It was time to begin the deepest healing, and it would not be an easy path. Although that strength had served her well, Spirit knew it was time to show the woman that it was no longer a tool to help her endure; rather, it had become her Destroyer. Her Lifelong Protector had become her Killer.

This Lesson proved to be extremely difficult for the woman in a way that the others had not. Her strength had woven itself into the very heart of her identity. She had worn it like a badge of honour. She, and all who knew her, had come to rely on this as an integral part of who she had become. It was terrifying to imagine what others would think of her if she were anything but always The Strong One.

Probably, most frightening of all was how it would alter her opinion of herself. She had always known herself so well, but she did not know who she would be at the end of the shedding of this self-destructive identity. The badge of honour had grown into a suit of armour, which was keeping her isolated not only from others, but from herself. It had cut off her ability to be all she was meant to be. It was keeping her from fully sharing and experiencing her Life, and her Self.

Somehow, she had to find a different kind of strength, the kind that would allow her to be weak, to need, to lean, to be dependent upon others. History had taught her of the danger in these, so it came as no surprise that she found herself facing a terrifying fork in the road. It seemed to her as though both of the two paths presented would be the death of her.

And in fact, this was quite true. She stood at the fork and gazed upon the Road of Familiarity, so dry and barren, brown and lifeless, knowing that Death stood waiting for her at the end of it. And as she peered cautiously down the Road of Change, she could see that it was overgrown with branches, lush and thick with leaves, hanging over the path, making it dark and impossible to see what was beyond the first bend.

Her heart skipped a beat; she was filled with fear, for Death stood waiting at the beginning of that road. To begin the journey along that path meant the Death of the Self she had come to know so well. Although she was aware that Re-Birth awaited her just beyond that bend, this was very frightening. She knew only how to be strong and independent.

It seemed inconceivable to her that she was deserving of the permission to also be weak, to be vulnerable, to need, since these had only yielded anger or rejection from others. She knew she had to find a balance between strength and weakness, that there was room for both, which would allow her to be a whole person with the frailties that she had always allowed others, but never herself.

She stood and pondered the two paths, fearful of traveling both. Contemplating the consequences of each journey, she moved toward the Road of Familiarity, which seemed much less frightening than the Road of Change.

Suddenly, Spirit burst forth, showing her that if she gave her power to Fear, and refused to walk the new and terrifying path, she would die.

And so, with one small and hesitant step, she chose Life, and gingerly set out to find it.

For many long years, the Keeper of the Stars had wandered through the Heavens, past the little Spirit's crystal star, watching in silent horror as the wounds appeared on it, one after another, after another. Some were caused when others inflicted hurt upon the dear Spirit, while others appeared when she hurt someone else or herself, even with just her thoughts

He remembered the gentle sweetness of the Spirit, the quiet strength that was truly remarkable, and the courage, which was well hidden behind the childlike innocence. Many times, he leaned against that once-perfect crystal star, and wept, his tears falling onto the crystal and dulling its formerly brilliant finish. He was certain that the Spirit would not be defeated, and that one day, there would be a radiant star in the Heavens, the likes of which were seldom seen.

But in the meantime, he was well aware of the suffering that was taking place in the little Spirit's Life. He could do nothing but wait for the turn-around he knew would come. And finally, that day arrived.

As the Spirit gained in strength, leading the woman down the Road of Change, the woman's journey of healing began. Slowly, some of the cracks, scratches and chips on the crystal began to disappear as she found understanding and hope.

It was a long and difficult process, but the woman kept working at it. The journey was not without its pitfalls, and there were times when it seemed as though the woman had not really learned the Lessons at all, falling back into the Old Ways, but still, she persevered. Although at times, it was one step forward, two steps backward, she carried on, Spirit taking the woman's hand and leading her on her healing journey.

As the woman remembered and relied on Spirit, the human element faded, giving way to her true essence and allowing her to find her Self. It was during this journey of healing that she found her way to forgiving the Father and yes, even the Mother as she began to understand their own pain and scars that had caused them to inflict so many terrible wounds on her. And she began to understand the pain that she had inflicted on them, too.

But the hardest part of that lesson still waited. She was not yet able to forgive herself.

God and Goddess were, of course, watching every step of the way, and they were delighted to see that this Child of Theirs had finally reached the point of beginning to heal. They smiled lovingly at each other, and at the woman, knowing that when she returned to them, she would be relating wonderful and powerful Lessons that had been learned.

When the Mother's Earthly Life was completed, her Spirit returned Home, where she was met by the Keeper of the Stars, and by God and Goddess, who were seated next to her crystal star which was so damaged, it was almost impossible to find any clear, untouched space on its surface. The Spirit of the Mother began to speak, and her tale was long and sad. She had seen hard times as a girl, and her Life had been a series of hardships and failures. Sadly, she had never managed to come to a place of healing. Hers was a very wounded Spirit, and because of this, she had wounded others, as well.

It was the usual practice during these Meetings that God and Goddess did not speak, for they did not wish to interfere with the flow of thought, and given that this was, in fact, like a test, they did not wish to give away any answers. They would always sit in silence, and let the Spirits speak until they were through.

And so it was that they sat and listened to the Mother, as she spoke defensively of her journey, her troubles, and how she had fulfilled her role in the lives of others.

The Mother's was such a young Spirit that even being back Home, she had trouble understanding what had happened in her Earthly Life. Quickly, it became evident that she was locked in the Human Life, and that she was struggling to reconnect with her Spirit, a struggle which had been apparent during her time on Earth, and one which had not been mastered.

The Old Man, God and Goddess well understood that she had done the best that she could, that the Lessons were not meant to be fully learned in this Life, and that they would still need to be learned in another.

In her Earthly Life, her need for power, control and domination had been motivated by her fear that she would be alone and unloved. In the Spirit world, all could see the irony in this, but in the Earthly realm, so many Humans suffered from the same fear, yet only the Oldest Souls knew how to overcome it. The answer came from having had many Lives, and learning many Lessons. And the answer came from the Purest of Love.

The Mother stood before the Old Man, the God and the Goddess, stumbling over her words as she attempted to reconnect with her Spirit. It was a lengthy and difficult Meeting, going through each of the wounds on her crystal. At first, she was extremely defensive, refusing to take responsibility for any of the pain she had inflicted on others, and therefore, on herself, as well.

Although it had been difficult to understand from a Human perspective, this Spirit was playing a necessary role in the Greater Plan. Everything needed to happen exactly as it had in order for others to complete their work. The Daughter needed the Mother Spirit to be exactly as she had been in her Earthly Life in order to master as many of her Lessons as she was meant to do in that Life. In this regard, even the youngest, least developed, and seemingly most destructive Souls still proved themselves to be excellent teachers.

As with the youngest Spirits, the Mother Spirit had been reluctant to let go of her Human form until the last possible moment, preferring to stay connected with the Earthly Realm, rather than to reconnect with her Higher Self. But finally, as she neared the completion of the accounting of her Life, the Mother Spirit began to let go of the Human body she had inhabited for so long, and as she did so, some of the Lessons came to her.

She was able to recount many loving and kind things that she had done, some of which were from her heart, others of which were created from her own wounds. She had a better understanding of all that had taken place, of the wounds she had endured, of how they had affected her and others, and she sought Forgiveness. She also found it in her heart to forgive those who had hurt her throughout her Life, including the Daughter, and saw the places where she could have progressed but had chosen not to do so, promising to consider those before her next Life.

The Spirit Within

The Keeper of the Stars was delighted when the Mother Spirit had reached this point, for her crystal was beginning to repair itself, and before the eyes of all who stood nearby, its clarity and brilliance were beginning to return. And in the same moment, there was a dramatic healing of the Daughter Spirit's crystal, and the crystals of many others, too.

The Mother's accounting finally complete, she turned to her crystal star. With one long, last look at God, Goddess and the Keeper of the Stars, she smiled, knowing that they loved her still. She stood, gazing at them, losing any last trace of her Earthly form, returning again to Pure Spirit.

Slowly, she began to swirl and spin, charging the crystal with her energy. Though it was not one of the largest or most radiant stars in the Heavens, there had been enough healing of the Mother's wounds, and enough understanding of the Lessons learned, that the crystal had been sufficiently repaired to produce a soft and gentle glow.

In time, she would again be given the chance to progress when she had done all the study and preparation necessary to leave the crystal, and seek further growth in another New Life. As was the case with all Spirits, she would continue to grow and learn, becoming a bigger and brighter star each time she returned Home.

In time, it was the Daughter's turn. She went Home to God and Goddess, her true Parents, where she stood facing them and the Keeper of the Stars for her reckoning. She always likened that part of the Homecoming to a final exam after many years' study and learning.

With outstretched arms, God and Goddess welcomed the Spirit, eager to embrace their Child after her long journey. They shared a few moments' silence, all simply enjoying being together once more. It was the little Spirit who was first to speak. She was barely able to contain many of the Lessons that had been learned while living the Life of the tormented little girl who grew into the damaged woman, and who then had become a woman who healed -- and not just her Self, but others as well.

Standing there in the presence of God, Goddess, and the Keeper of the Stars, she still bore the shape and the face of that woman, as Spirits always did when they first arrived back Home, still connected to their Human experience on the Earthly Plane.

She spoke of the loneliness at first, since this was the first consciousness she had experienced in this Life. "I was so lost," she said. "I didn't belong anywhere. I felt as though I was not loved, and my very survival was threatened right from the first moment. It was as if I had been cut off, even from myself. I was all wrong.

"These were the messages I got from the people I had chosen as my parents, and it took me many years to begin to unravel why I would have made such a choice. Of course, I did not remember my past Lives, so I had no idea why I was continually ending up in situations which only served to confirm those beliefs, and which threatened my life and my Soul."

To the rapt audience , it seemed as though the thoughts were bubbling up and spilling forth in words she could no longer contain. She had the attention of the Old Man, as well as her Creators, as she continued with excitement. "In this Life, I chose four parents, each of whom would contribute in various ways to the learning I was ultimately meant to do. The first two laid the foundations for the lessons I was meant to learn.

"But it was my adopted family that taught me the rest of what would set me up properly for my Life's Learning. I was not allowed to have any control or feelings. I was taught that I was not important to anyone. I was stripped of my ability to express myself, and I was criticized, insulted and shamed daily. I was expected to be dutiful and obedient. I was considered unacceptable as myself. I was told I did not deserve good things, and I was subjected to a lot of violence, and violation.

"There was a Father, and although he contributed to the difficulties I had, in time he and I made our peace. The hurting stopped and he showed me nothing but love and acceptance for many years. I had forgiven him for the pain he had caused me, and for having so many of his own wounds, he was unable to protect me from my Mother. It had taken me a long time to understand that if he had protected me, I would not have learned so many of the Lessons. It was exactly as it needed to be, and for that, I am grateful.

"I remembered that for all his flaws and the damage he had caused me, he had been the only one who had still managed to show me love and concern throughout those difficult years I was growing up.

"But I hadn't been able to notice any of it for many long years because of the overwhelming negativity surrounding me. Any good he was able to do had been overshadowed, outweighed, suffocated by the toxic black cloud that was swallowing my very Soul. But then, this, too, carried significant Lessons for me, Lessons that I was finally able to learn."

Her eyes misted, and she recalled the human experience of being a daughter whose father, the only person who ever showed her any love as a child, had died.

God and Goddess looked knowingly at one another, remembering how she relied on them during the last days of the Father's Life. They well remembered the Daughter's struggles of Human experience versus Spiritual Being throughout that period. They heard her pleas for strength; they heard her confusion, asking for the Father to be taken, to stop his suffering; and then they heard her acknowledge knowing that to ask this was taking away the Father's Free Will.

At some points, through her loving tears, she said she no longer cared about that; the Father hurt so much, she just wanted it to stop. She wanted to pray like other people and just ask for him to be taken Home. But always, she recanted immediately, knowing that it was wrong to attempt to alter the course of one of the most important events in the Father's own Life and Lessons, and knowing that it would ultimately alter hers, as well, if she did that.

Instead, she pondered what she was meant to learn from this difficult experience, remembering that this Human event was another opportunity for Spiritual growth. She continued to ask for strength to get through it all, and she asked to be allowed to be with the Father when he crossed over, since he had indicated to the Daughter that this was his wish.

The Old Man thought back to that time, and remembered how the little Spirit's crystal star was cracking like never before, and that suddenly, very late one night, a huge piece of it shattered, sending tiny shards flying in several directions. It was the moment the Daughter, who had been lying with her head on her Father's chest, heard the escape of one long last breath and realised there would not be another.

Indeed, it had been one of the most difficult times in the woman's Life, but it was because she loved her Father so. She was going to miss his physical presence, being held in the warm embrace of her Father's arms, feeling the love in her Father's smile. She also realised that the amount of pain she experienced was equal to the amount of love she felt, and in that knowledge, was content to bear the hurt of losing her beloved Father. He was the only one who fed the girl's starving Soul at times during the darkness of her young life. And for much of the rest of the years they had together, it had been the same.

She used to wonder why the Father had been unable to keep her safe from the Mother, but after a time, she had come to understand that she had chosen it to be this way for many reasons. Part of the Spiritual Lesson was about learning to stand up for herself, which had proven to be one of her longest and most difficult battles. It was a Lesson that was learned a wee bit at a time, in little steps over a very long period. It would have been impossible for her make any progress, had there always been someone there, protecting her.

The Spirit continued. "This family also gave me the opportunity to work on Self-worth and Self-love. I struggled with these Lessons for a very long time, and they were among the most complicated to unravel. It should not be so hard to love the Self, given that it is so easy to love and value others. It is one of the most essential elements to living a happy and healthy Human Life. Without truly loving and honouring the Self, the Human Life suffers physically, mentally, and emotionally, because it is actually a Spiritual condition of starvation and of withering. And that is where I lived for much of this Life, unable to feel the kind of love and respect for my Self that I felt for others.

"For many years, I thought that my struggle with this was a purely Human one, that my Human Self had been so deeply wounded after repeatedly being given messages about my not being valuable, lovable, deserving of anything good. After a time, I came to believe that it was a Human problem that could be remedied in the Spiritual realm.

"But one day, I was struck by the most profound insight. I understood that it was not my Human Self that was wounded, or carrying the pain; it was my Spirit, and it needed healing. It was a much deeper injury than I had ever imagined. I had always thought that all the pain we experienced as Humans was simply on that level, wounding us emotionally, and that all the hurts of an Earthly Life could be healed by connecting with our Spiritual selves. But I was wrong.

"In that Life, I realised that we choose our Earthly Lives and our Lessons before we inhabit a body, and are meant to learn and grow as Spirits. I thought of all Human experience as contributing to Spiritual Lessons, and sought to find the lesson in the difficult parts of my Earthly Life. It took many years, and many terrible times before I understood that as Spirits, we, too, can be wounded, battered, and broken.

"When Human troubles flare, a person will often seek guidance and strength by turning to a Spiritual Source outside himself. He does not understand that in reality, he is reconnecting with his own Spirit, which is the true source of healing.

"You, our True Parents, God and Goddess who created us, are always here for us, but it is not the two of You who do the healing work or provide the strength we need in our Earthly Lives. Your role is to show us Perfect Love, teaching it by your example. It is that Love which sustains us, as Human and Spirit work together to heal the Self.

"However, there are times when the wounds are too deep, and Spirit is well hidden, seemingly out of reach. The Spirit, or Soul, is beaten and bruised, and a profound healing of it is necessary. If it does not happen, the physical body will become sick and die, for it manifests all that is the Spirit. It is Spirit which gives Life and Energy, and it is Spirit which takes them away.

"How often do we listen to Humans say 'The body is not really the person, it is the Spirit or the Soul that defines him or her'? They say the body is just a vessel to contain the Spirit, a means by which the Spirit fulfills its purpose. We hear them say such things especially when they are contemplating death. And to an extent, they are correct.

"However, they are missing a vitally important point. The body is so much more than a mechanical vessel; every cell becomes empowered by the Spirit, by the Life Force. It is a perfect marriage of the physical and the Spiritual, the deepest kind of interconnectedness possible. One cannot exist without the other. It is like a Perfect Circle of the Divine, which is expressed when a Spirit inhabits a human body. We also experience this Perfect and Divine Circle when we consummate a loving relationship, expressing the Spirit's pure love in a physical way, binding the two realms.

"No, the body is not merely a vessel for the Spirit. They are symbiotically connected. There are times when the Spirit is too deeply injured, and the Life Force is not sufficient to carry on. The physical body cannot maintain wholeness and integrity when it houses a deeply wounded Spirit. It is entirely affected by the Spirit, and will manifest all that Spirit is."

Once again, the Spirit paused, deep in thought for a time, reflecting on how it came to be that she learned this Lesson. The Old Man, the God and the Goddess waited patiently until she was ready to continue.

"Further, as with most problems and obstacles of an Earthly Life, they are just more Lessons that the Spirit is learning through Human experience, and therefore, they can only be overcome by Spiritual means. Too often, Humans look outside themselves for answers. They seek to blame someone for their difficulties and frailties, rather than looking inside, which will direct them to the Heavens, and which will then lead them back to the Divine, the Higher Purpose, the Reason For All Things. As difficult as their lives can be, it must be so in order for them to learn the Lessons that they chose.

"And so it was in the families I selected. I knew what it would be when I made the decision, and you knew it when I sought your approval for this Life. But as you know, we no longer remember those choices once we are there, and stumble along until some part of the Spirit shines through to remind us of the Divine. Then the real Learning begins, the Learning of the Spirit, the reason for the whole experience at all.

"I had many very hard lessons to learn, and as painful and difficult as the experience was, I am grateful for all of it, for it was an excellent opportunity to learn those Lessons which I finally did complete. And this, of course, was the point of the entire exercise. I entered those families not only as a student, but also as a teacher.

"It is such a complicated process, isn't it, how we all choose our Human Lives to work out our Spiritual Lessons, and the choice is made in an interconnected, intertwining way, involving many others. All of us begin our Human Lives, knowing full well what we will encounter, and who will be in our Lives, and what we are meant to learn during our precious days on Earth. It appears to Humans as though some people waste a Life, seeming to refuse to learn while they are there; yet that is all a valuable part of the Greater Plan. It is meant to be exactly the way it is."

She paused, reflecting. "There is just so much to tell; there were far more Lessons in this Life than I could begin to relate to you. I have told you some of the most important ones, the ones that were truly Life-Altering for me, but there are more that I must share with you.

"After years of pain and difficulty, and searching for something without knowing what it was, I realised that I had been wasting valuable time and energy, trying to find a Human being to fix my need for love and belonging, until finally, I understood that this was a Spiritual Lesson, which began when I was unwanted at conception. I tolerated abuse and unhappiness in the name of love until eventually I understood that no Human being could, or even should attempt to fix my Spiritual issues for me.

"I realised that as a Spiritual Being, I needed to reconnect with the Source of all Love, my true Parents, my true Creators, God and Goddess. In fact, that was how I would find healing: through Perfect Love. One of the most powerful Lessons in reconnecting with my Creators was to understand that I had always been Loved, even when I did not feel it because of all the Human conditions surrounding me. Nor had I ever been alone, yet I had felt that way all of my Life until that point.

"After that day, I spent a fair amount of time, casting Sacred Circles in which I remembered and visited with you, my true Parents, allowing myself to feel your love, and your comforting. Each time, it was a bittersweet reunion, having been away so long, but also being very happy to be back in the embrace of those who knew me, accepted me, and loved me completely, for all I was, and despite all I was not.

"From that point on, I was much more able to remember my Spirit and to honour it. I had been trying to live a more Spiritual lifestyle before that time, but there were dramatic improvements in my ability to do so after that. I looked at everything differently, and especially, all of the relationships I had with friends, family, romantic partners, even colleagues. I saw the ways in which so many Human frailties make themselves evident in all types of relationships, and how it is very difficult to have a truly loving and nurturing relationship of any kind with anyone, when there is no

Spiritual basis for it, or no Spiritual connection or link for either party.

"I learned that I allowed others to strip me of my confidence because of their opinions of me. It took years of pain and heartache to understand that this is a Human issue with many Spiritual Lessons attached. One of these has to do with judgement, and understanding that although as Human beings, we sometimes tend to fall into this behaviour, it is another Lesson for the Spirit to realise that it comes from a lack of Spiritual awareness and growth.

"Allowing myself to be affected by someone in that state was only Self-destructive; it served no useful purpose. Another's opinion is not necessarily based in fact, yet as Humans, we tend to forget that, and make decisions about ourselves and the world around us, simply based on what another person believes to be the truth. We do not honour the Spirit when we make such choices; rather, we destroy it.

"In this Life, I had numerous Lessons to do with Self-destruction; that was one which I was happy to recognise and release when it came to me. Judgement comes from insecurities and other wounds. There is no place for such behaviour in a relationship between Divinely Inspired Spirits. It makes no sense to Self-destruct over someone else's refusal to learn Spiritual Lessons.

"There comes a time when Humans must realize that their belief systems were largely created by others' opinions of them as they were growing up, and that they will continually seek out people who will validate those beliefs, even after they have become adults.

"But a belief system can be changed. Beliefs are fed to us because they came from others. Worse than that, they do not even have to be people we know, love, or trust. A belief system is not necessarily based in fact, and is open to a complete re-evaluation, throwing out the toxic beliefs that are invalid, and rebuilding our beliefs based on facts and ideals. Only then can we live in Truth as our Higher Selves."

Spirit was lost in thought for a time. Finally, she spoke once more. "Another of the most important Lessons I learned in this Life was that we must understand that we have no control over what someone else's thoughts might be. It does not matter who we are or what we do, ultimately another person's opinion is his or her own business and we cannot control it, although too often, we will try, or sometimes will even take responsibility for it.

"As well, the moment we allow other people's opinions, or even our fear of their opinions, to influence any choices we make, or how we feel about ourselves, we have given them our power and our control, even if they are unaware of it, even if they did not ask for it, even if they never abuse it. We have given up ourselves, and are then operating from a position of fear, doubt and insecurity. Coming from such a place, it is impossible to function at our best. That is, as our Highest Selves.

"And the worst of this is that it is of our own making; if we allow this, we are not in a place of self-love or self-respect, because in doing so, we have handed over our Selves to these peope, and again, even if those people are unaware. It is the ultimate in giving up control when we do it without others even *attempting* to take it.

"This issue raises another. Much earlier in this Life, I had learned that there is no room for control in any relationship, other than self-control. I thought I had become quite good at functioning without being controlling, at least, not in the usual unhealthy ways about which I had learned.

But at this particular point in my journey, when I was digging deeply into myself in my search for understanding and Spiritual growth, I also saw a very subtle, yet powerful form of control in relationships, which I had never seen before, and which completely surprised me.

"This kind of control is seen when Humans are restrictive of another person, under the guise of being concerned about his or her health and well-being. If a husband, for example, is being restricted by his wife in terms of what he may or may not eat, drink, or otherwise ingest, she may insist that it is because she is worried about him, which, in her mind, may well be the case.

"However, it is still his choice, his Lessons that ultimately end up being affected. It is not love in its highest and purest form. In fact, it is not based in love at all. It is based in fear. And she is not learning her lessons about this either.

"And although it looks relatively innocuous, and can even appear to be helpful and loving behaviour, it is actually quite destructive. When we inhabit Human bodies, we do tend to live a very Human experience. After all, that is the point, of course. It can become difficult to find or remember the Spiritual Path, and because it is sometimes less demanding to live in the Humanness than in our Highest Selves, it can be very easy to slip into Human ways of thinking, behaving and connecting.

"In this example of a wife's concern for her husband's health, it is easy for her to say she loves him and does not want him to die because he did not take care of himself. And it is easy for him to go along with it to please her, or because he is afraid to die. Or maybe he goes along with it out of respect for her because he loves her.

"But think about his Lessons in all of those possibilities. If he does as she says, just to please her, there is an obvious Lesson he is missing in making that decision. Why does he need to please her? That is going to be a Spiritual Lesson, and he is missing the opportunity to learn it. Or what if it is because he is afraid to die? The answer is the same. And as well, if he does it because he loves her, then once again, he is missing the Lesson.

"If he is going to do it at all, it should be because he is doing it for himself, out of respect for his own body, his own health and well-being, and of course, only he should be worrying about his Spiritual Lessons, for only he can recognise and master them.

"It does not matter what the reason for the wife's behaviour may be; the fact remains that in this example, the husband is being asked to change. Whether the wife truly believes that it is for his own good, and it is out of love for him, it is about her need to have some control over him to alleviate her own fears or needs. There is nothing selfless in it at all, not really.

"It is about her wanting to be with him, being afraid to lose him, being afraid of his death, or afraid of being on her own, or any number of other things. But none of the wife's actions or the husband's responses is about love. All of them are entirely about issues with fear and control. So ultimately, not only is she interfering with his Karmic Lessons, she is missing the opportunity to master some of her own as well.

"Interestingly, as Spirits, we love to change. We love to learn. It is part of our purpose! Yet when we take Human form, the point of which is to allow us that learning, we become terrified of change, terrified of growth. And worse, as Humans, none of us wants to be told to change to please someone else, yet we think nothing of expecting someone else to change to suit us. That is a huge injustice to all concerned. It is an injustice on the most basic level of Human love and respect, but it is a much larger injustice on the Spiritual level."

There was a pensive look across the sensitive face for a few moments before the Spirit continued.

"One of my favourite Life-Altering, Soul-Saving Lessons came not long after that one. I was continuing my deepening self-discovery and awareness, and had come up against a particularly trying time in that Life. Since I could not remember my choices from this side, I had begun to question my Lessons and my Destiny.

"I had begun to wonder whether I was destined only to struggle, because it seemed that no matter how I worked to try to make things better, I kept ending up in the same lonely place, enduring abusive or toxic relationships, never finding real love, for which I had been searching for as long as I could remember. I believed that everything happens exactly the way it is meant to do; therefore, I began to think that it did not matter what I did, I was not destined to be happy.

"I had also always believed that there was still room for Free Will and Choice, although at that point, I had not got very far in trying to figure out how they fit with Things Meant To Be. I felt the need to begin a fairly lengthy Self-analysis. Not like the ones we do here, of course; Humans' ability to comprehend the Spiritual only goes so far. But I made my first reasonable attempt at it for that Life, and I was really quite surprised by the answers that came to me.

"As I examined the major turning points in that Life, I tore apart each choice. I was quite ruthless about it, because I knew I would get nowhere if I could not be completely honest with myself. I was determined to understand why I had made the major choices that had significantly altered the course of my Life. Eventually, I saw a common thread running through each choice, and although it should not really have shocked me, for some reason, it did.

"What I saw was fear. It had been the driving force behind every major choice I had made until that time. And even worse, in most of those cases, at the times I made those choices, I was well aware of its toxic presence, prompting and pushing me, sometimes even swallowing me whole. On each of those occasions, I was unable to comprehend fully how it would ultimately affect me, or what it would come to mean in the course of my Life.

"I went one step further in my efforts to understand on the deepest possible level what had been taking place in my Life, or at least, the deepest that I was meant to go at that point. When I examined the fear, I saw that it went back to my first human consciousness in that Life, at the moment of my conception, the fear for my survival because I was unwanted and unloved by everyone but my young mother.

"That Lesson was repeated over and over again during that Life, and it was not until that experience of self-analysis that I became aware of how profoundly and negatively that same fear had affected me."

The Spirit stopped for a few moments, and it seemed as though she were replaying some of these events in her mind. A sweet, sorrowful expression appeared briefly on her face, while she paused to consider her own words.

She continued, "I realised once again that I had been misguided in my efforts to stop feeling fear. Of course, in reality, I was only running from it. In fact, it seemed to grow, the fear feeding itself, taking on a life of its own. It seemed the more I tried to hide from it, the more fearful situations presented themselves.

"Foolishly, I did not understand that to avoid them did not mean I could avoid the fear, itself. It followed me everywhere I went until that day, and with some horror, I realised that I had given it much of my Life. Finally, I decided to stop running. I turned around, planted my feet firmly in the ground and looked Fear in the eye. I challenged it. I wanted -- no, I *demanded* that it give back my Life. I will not pretend that I did not still experience Fear after that moment; however, I refused to allow it any more power. I refused to give it any more of my Life."

The three listeners were intrigued. All of them smiled as they felt the strength that Spirit had gained with this Lesson, strength that was no longer Self-destructive, strength that was about beginning to achieve Wholeness and Healing. They remembered well what she had written about this extremely difficult Lesson when she applied for this particular Life. They knew how important this was, what it meant to this Spirit

She continued. "Once I stopped letting Fear stop me, my Life improved dramatically. I was overwhelmed by how many facets of it were changed for the better. It gave me freedom! It was as though someone had handed me an entirely new Life. I took risks in relationships, daring to speak my Truth, despite the possible consequences.

"No longer did I fear my vulnerability; I was able to shed my Self-destructive image of infallible strength. There was great healing just in that alone. I had many wonderful, exciting, experiences that I would never have had before, putting myself in what I perceived to be terrifying situations that usually proved to be absolutely simple or exhilarating, exciting, or joyful. It was the first taste of real freedom I had in this Life. Indeed, it was very empowering."

With a far-away look in her eyes, a peaceful expression crossed the Spirit's face, and a gentle little smile followed. She was quiet for a few moments, remembering the releasing of Fear.

"My hard-fought battle with Fear led me to a clearer vision of another Lesson which had been evident throughout my Life. This was the Lesson of Letting Go. Until that time, I had thought of them as separate Lessons.

"But in time, I reached a point where I saw them as connected. I was very small when I understood that I was going to have to let go of a lot in my Life, and rather than accept this, I fought hard to hold on, out of a deep need for security, stability, and of course, love. To let go was terrifying. I held on to material things for the comfort or the memories they offered. I held on to beliefs, to relationships, to anything that seemed to fill a part of the deep yearning and longing which I had always known.

"To learn this Lesson meant facing my Fear of Letting Go. It meant recognising and letting go of the Self-destructive behaviours and the Human needs that were driving them. It meant one of the longest climbs to connecting with my Highest Self, and of course, as you are well aware, was one of the times I relied most heavily on you, my Divine Creators. I could feel your Love and Strength very powerfully during those days, reminding me that as long as I walked Your Path, the journey would not be as arduous as I feared.

"There were many occasions in my Life which offered me the opportunity to learn about Letting Go, so it was not an unfamiliar companion. The difference on the occasion of understanding its connection to Fear was that I was forced to examine it and learn it in a much deeper fashion.

"I thought about the substantial amount of time I had spent feeling unable to let go of the Past and wishing I could change many parts of it. How long I had dreamed of reliving previous experiences, in the hopes of putting them right. I wasted so much time looking behind me, revisiting where I had already been, that often, I did not notice the path I was on, much less the road ahead. In doing this, I missed much of my Life, and in that moment of realisation, I was given yet another opportunity to stop wasting another moment of it. What a blessing!"

The Spirit paused for a very long time at this point, reflecting most thoughtfully. The three listeners sat patiently in silence, allowing her the time she needed before she carried on.

"Once again, I was struck by the way the Lessons fit together, for as I began work in earnest, learning to let go, I came face to face with one Lesson which I had been avoiding for a very long time. It was the Lesson of Forgiveness. I felt its sting, like salt in an open wound, raw and burning every time it crossed my mind. I had been hurt by a few people on such a profoundly deep Spiritual level that I did not think I could ever heal, and I was certain I would never forgive them. I needed to hang on to the hatred and the anger for more than one reason. In part, I believed it would be a betrayal of my Self if I were to forgive them. But there was more -- more that I did not wish to see.

"Although I was well aware that I was the only one being hurt by my unforgiving heart, I felt justified in holding onto the anger, and I did not care if it was hurting me. It seemed right and necessary.

"Years passed before I understood that these people would never understand how they had affected me; nor was it likely that they would ever care. I realised that in all likelihood, they were probably giving me very little thought at all - if any.

"Meanwhile, I was filled with toxic, destructive hatred and anger for these people, refusing to forgive them for what I perceived were their sins against me, not wanting to accept that I was doing myself far more harm than they had ever done to me.

"When finally, I was able to release the hatred and the anger that I held in my heart, and to replace it with forgiveness, this was another enormous gift of Freedom for myself. Although they were unaware of it, this was also a gift to them, because until that day, my Spirit was creating negative energy that was sent to them without my notice. Once I learned this aspect of Forgiveness, and the energy in my life became more positive, it could only do good things for them, and for me.

"It took me a very long time to accept that the situations with these people were also Spiritual Lessons, and to accept that they were Meant To Be, that I had chosen them before I requested this Life, and that all of the people involved were doing exactly what they were meant to do. It was all a part of the Greater Plan. All of those concerned had Lessons to learn; everything was connected.

"My anger was futile; it served no purpose. Its only result was destructive to all concerned, as no Human resolution was ever possible in either of those situations. Rather, they required Spiritual resolution, because they were designed to be a part of our Spiritual learning.

"I saw how deeply I had been hurting my Self, both on the physical level and in the Spiritual realm, as well. I was creating a toxic environment for my body, and I was not allowing my Spirit to be free to grow and learn. I had put my Self in chains. And directing negative energy at these people was also keeping them in chains, which was not only detrimental to my own progress, but to theirs as well. I finally understood that I had to let it all go. All of us had Lessons to learn. I had no right to prevent or interfere with that. It was when I saw my refusal to 'let go' and forgive that I saw the connection between these two valuable Lessons.

"I feel I must add that the Mother was not one of those whom I hated, for I knew that she was one of my most important teachers.

Probably, she was *the* most important one of all. Because of her, I was given the opportunity to learn some of my greatest Lessons, which ultimately enriched my Life and helped me to fulfill my purpose on Earth. I struggled for a long time, however, until I reached this place of understanding, which included understanding that she, too, was a very wounded Soul.

"We were, in fact, quite similar in one respect; each of us had hurt the other, as a result of the injuries to our own Spirits. For years afterward, I longed to have this conversation with her, and to tell her of my learning, and of my love and appreciation for her as a Spiritual being, despite the great pain I had felt as her Human daughter. I wanted to tell her that although I had not intended it, I had also caused her pain in my Life, and to ask her Forgiveness, and to explain all of this to her.

"However, I knew she was a very Young Spirit. It was another occasion for me to let go of my Earthly needs, and to remember my Spiritual Lessons. I was well aware that she had not progressed enough in her own learning to be able to hear or appreciate my words. But she will now."

And far away, the Mother's crystal star suddenly began to shine more brightly, as very many of its scars were healed due to the appreciation, understanding, and love of the Daughter, and for the giving and the desire for forgiveness.

"What I also came to realise," she continued, "was that there are two other aspects of Forgiveness that are vital to our happiness and our well-being, to our healing. We must also learn to ask forgiveness when we have hurt others, because if we have caused pain, it is essential to the healing of others to know that we understand what we did, and it is essential to our own growth, as we realise where we went wrong, and do our best to avoid causing further pain.

"In all of the Lessons to do with Forgiveness, I found that the hardest one was to forgive myself. I was my own worst enemy. No one could have made me feel more remorse for my mistakes than I. And even when others had forgiven me, even when I had not gone nearly as wrong as I had thought, I still struggled to forgive myself. It took many long years before I could do this, always having expected perfection from myself, but from no one else, even though I knew I could not master it.

"And when I did not live up to my expectations of myself, when I felt I had failed myself or others, I thought that not only were my actions unforgivable, but I was, as well. In trying to understand why I felt that way, it eventually became evident to me that my inability to forgive my Self was wrapped up in my first conscious moment as a human; I was not worthy of living or of being loved. Therefore, I could not possibly be worthy of forgiveness.

"As I contemplated the Lessons I had learned regarding Fear, Letting Go, and Forgiveness, and having been led back to my earliest pain in this human Life, I saw very clearly another Lesson which had been trying to surface for some time. Although I had managed a small amount of progress with it in some areas of my Life, I could see at this juncture that it was of a magnitude that I found to be overwhelming. I had been struggling with the Lesson of Acceptance throughout my life, with each fearful moment, with each occasion of having to let go of someone or something I loved. I believed that all conditions of life serve a Higher Purpose, yet I had not managed total Acceptance of this idea.

"As I tried to understand what was creating this obstacle, my eyes were opened to another facet of the Lesson of Fear. As I have described to you, once I saw how much I had let Fear control my Life, I refused to allow this any longer. I began making choices, in spite of Fear, rather than because of it. I learned that having courage does not mean being Fearless, but instead, it means having the Fear and facing it, rather than attempting to run or hide from it.

"Once I reached the Lesson of Acceptance, and searched inside my Self to determine why I seemed unable to master it, I saw that I had only learned the Lesson of Facing Fear in terms of situations over which I had some control. It was in decisions and choices that I had come to believe I had mastered it. In this way, I had conquered and released many fears, or when I still felt it, I refused to allow it to be part of my decision-making process.

"However, I suddenly realised that I still felt an enormous amount of Fear about situations over which I had no control. I feared that my husband would die. I feared that I would develop a terrible illness and be subjected to great pain and suffering. I feared for the long-term safety and well being of my Self and the people I loved.

"It was then that I saw what was holding me back, and how these pieces of the puzzle fit together. I could not control these things, so they frightened me. And this Fear led me back to the Lesson of Letting Go, and I was aware of yet another way in which I needed to reinforce that Lesson.

"Suddenly, I could see one of the most important Lessons that until that point, I had not yet fully understood. It was vital to all the others. It played a significant part in the unfolding and piecing together of a Lifetime of learning. I had neglected a monumental part of the entire picture. It was in the Lesson of Trust."

Spirit paused for a moment, having grown rather serious, and was quiet. Her listeners were intrigued, wanting to hear more, but allowing the silence.

"For most of this Life, I had trusted in people and Earthly situations entirely too much. Repeatedly, my trust was betrayed, and I ended up deeply wounded. Because of my Human need to be loved, I gave my trust freely to anyone who would have it, and many who did not deserve it. In considering that I had always been a most trusting person, and thought I had mastered that particular Lesson, I failed to understand how it fit with the rest of my learning, especially with regard to the issue of Acceptance.

"And that is when the lightning bolt hit! My trust had been entirely misplaced! How could I have so freely trusted in imperfect Humans and in Earthly situations created by them, while at the same time, have difficulty placing trust in the Greater Plan, and in God and Goddess, in their Divine Wisdom and Grace? I truly believed that all conditions of life served a Higher Purpose, so why did I struggle with trusting the Divine Creators of All Things?

"I was overwhelmed by the power in this understanding, and by its simplicity as well. It may have been that until that time, the little child deep in my Soul was remembering all the parents who abandoned her in one form or another, creating my ability to trust only in relationships over which I had some measure of control. My attachments to my True Parents had been broken for many years, as I limped along and worked at healing them.

"It was not until those attachments had become strong and clear that I recognised that they had always been -- and always would be -- here to support me and to love me through whatever lay ahead. After a misguided and decades long search, I had finally found Perfect Trust.

"Along with this came an even greater release and Letting Go, as I felt all of those related issues begin to crumble and dissipate. No longer did I have room for even the smallest measure of trying to control what was out of my hands. So many fears and Human needs just melted away, as I remembered Perfect Trust.

"And as these pieces of the puzzle came together, I saw another, quietly moving in and taking its rightful place amongst the rest."

Spirit's eyes danced, and she smiled a wide and peaceful smile that warmed the hearts of those in her company. Eager to share more, she went on excitedly.

"Having finally understood the Lesson of Perfect Trust, I was suddenly struck by the realisation that Letting Go and Trusting in the Greater Plan must naturally lead to the Lesson of Acceptance. Once again, I was amazed by simplicity in this. The feeling of Freedom that washed over me in that moment was incredibly powerful and Life-Giving! I shall never forget it.

"In that moment, I understood that Perfect Trust resulted in Perfect Acceptance of What Was Meant To Be, which included all conditions of Life. I did, however, discover that the Lesson of Acceptance was not quite so simple, in and of itself, for it carried with it more than just one part. Although I had long before learned Acceptance of others, I had struggled continually with the hardest of all, Acceptance of Self. But then, the answer came to me. I knew what had been missing, what made accepting my Self so difficult. It had been impossible without Pefect Love.

"I will not forget the clarity with which suddenly I saw so many Lessons fall into place at once. It was truly a defining moment in my Life, after years of difficult struggle and trying to make sense of so many disjointed parts and Lessons, and all of it was right there before me, one leading to the next, which led to the next...I could not believe I had been unable to see it all before; it was just too simple! There they were, Perfect Love, Perfect Trust, and Perfect Acceptance, each requiring the others; a Divine Trinity, all that we really need."

Spirit smiled, and slowly shook her head from side to side, seeming to gently chide herself for having taken so long to understand.

After a few moments, she shifted her focus from remembering that moment, and she continued, eager to further explain.

"My healing journey was, of course, very long, and happened in little pieces at a time. I had been taking my Life apart and examining it closely as I tried to understand and improve it. Of course, one of the most difficult struggles I had was with relationships with partners. I had made much progress in healing the spiritual issues that had arisen in that area, and finally I met a man who seemed too good to be true.

"Over and over again, he showed me unconditional love. Never did he judge or criticise. He supported and encouraged me, and everything I needed to do, or was meant to be.

"He was patient and truly cared about me, and respected me. He did not have to agree with my thoughts or my deeds, but he would always accept them, as he did me. He had the purest heart and soul of anyone I had ever met. He showed me as perfect a love, and as perfect a trust as any Human Being ever could. This man seemed to know how to live only in his Highest Self. He was truly very directly connected with his Divine Spirit.

"Many years earlier, I left the Spirit World to begin my Human experience, in which I was meant to learn about Perfect Love, Perfect Trust, and Perfect Acceptance. From the beginning of my Human Life, I believed these did not exist in my world. But throughout the course of my Life and my learning, I came to understand that I had always had them from You, my Beloved Parents. And because of your pure and abiding love for me, I was able to experience a Human relationship that was based on the example of yours. This beautiful marriage was a very powerful expression of the Divine, of everything to which we should aspire during our Human Lives. I saw, in our marriage, a Human reflection of You, Beloved God and Goddess, and your Perfect Love, Trust and Acceptance. I had ended where I had begun: from the Spirit Realm, to the Earthly Life, and back again, a perfect demonstration of Spiritual Being having Human experience; the Spiritual Realm on Earth. I had found my way Home."

Once more, Spirit wore a far-away expression, and her eyes grew misty as she remembered her husband, and recalled their parting. It was something she could not begin to describe. She had so cherished their time together; his great love for her could be felt, even had he never spoken a word of it. It was as pure and perfect a love and a union as she could have ever imagined.

She knew that she was gradually moving away from her Earthly connections, and these were the last Human thoughts she would have of her sweet husband. And although she knew she would always remember him in the Spirit World, it would never be in the same way as she did now, while still in touch with the Earthly Realm. Therefore, she chose to keep sacred and private, her last thoughts as his wife.

It was a pensive Spirit who paced back and forth, a few slow steps, considering what next to say. It seemed to the listeners that she was about to make her summation. They waited patiently for her to begin to speak once again.

"Even when the Human element is strongly connected with the Spirit, the Lessons feel so hard on Earth. Before we are Master Spirits, we will tell each other as Humans that we would not appreciate the good parts of Life without the bad. But that is only because all the Lessons have not yet been learned. Here in the

Spirit Realm, we know what it will be someday, but they cannot yet understand. Only when we have mastered all the Lessons that God and Goddess have to teach us, and when we are filled with Divine Wisdom and Love, will there be a deep appreciation for the Earthly Life in its perfect state -- a state that imperfect Humans cannot grasp.

"But it really is just so simple, all of it. If only they knew...I long for the day when all Human suffering and frailty will be gone. The symbiotic relationship between Spirit and Human will be a dance of Perfection. With no more Spiritual wounds, there will be no disease or illness of body, mind or emotions. When the Earthly Life is done, there will be a simple and painless shedding of the Human body. Spirits will continue to choose New Lives, but not for the purpose of Learning. It will be for the purpose of enjoying the fruits of their labours in previous Lives while they were completing the Wheel of Learning.

"With all Human life being expressed in the perfection of Master Spirits, the world will be a Paradise like nothing ever imagined by people before. All Spirits will have finally learned all possible Lessons, and will live as Humans in their Highest Selves, creating Heaven on Earth, with complete Peace and Tranquility, and in the Purest Love."

The Creators and the Old Man were beaming. Clearly, many Lessons had been learned, and this Spirit was going to be ready for many more difficult challenges in the future. They were happy to have her back Home, and were very pleased for her regarding her significant accomplishments.

The time had come to accompany her Creators and the Old Man to her crystal star, the Mirror of her Soul, where she would remain, pondering the Lessons she had learned in this Life, waiting until it was time for her next.

As the group drifted through the Heavens, Spirit lost all resemblance to Human form. Upon reaching the crystal, there was only the Spirit in all its purity.

The Goddess looked lovingly at Spirit and said, "You have done well with your Lessons. Go now and be a source of Light and Inspiration for the other Spirits, as you ponder your learnings, your teachings, and as you prepare for yet another Life in the future."

God and Goddess embraced Spirit, as did the Keeper of the Stars. Spirit then stood in front of the large crystal, just like that day so long ago at the beginning of the Life that was just completed. Facing the others, arms outstretched to them in love, the Spirit glowed quietly.

Turning back toward the star, the Spirit began to swirl around it, slowly at first, then faster and faster, gradually shining brighter in the night sky. The cracks, scratches, and scrapes began to vanish almost instantly, restoring the great crystal, as her radiant energy once again engulfed the beautiful star. It was in this that Spirit's Lessons were most evident, for it was in the Lessons learned, and in the forgiveness for which she had asked and received, that the healing took place.

Suddenly, with a flash that illuminated the Heavens, she was inside the crystal, shining brilliantly in the night sky. And as her essence radiated across the Universe, the dimly lit stars of the Spirits who had so wounded her, and who she had wounded, too, began to shine a little more brightly, as her forgiveness of them, and theirs of her, healed the damage that had been done to their own crystals.

And now, when you look up into a clear night sky, you can search among the very brightest stars, and know that it is one of these that is this gentle and loving Spirit, pondering Lessons learned, still teaching other Spirits through its brilliant radiance, yet still a student, contemplating the many challenges and Lessons to come. One day, this Spirit would shine brighter still.

The Spirit Within

ABOUT THE AUTHOR

liberty forrest (who spells her name in lower case for a reason) was born in Regina, SK and moved to Calgary, AB at the age of 8. A painful, abusive childhood pushed her to leave home at 16 and embark on a rather turbulent personal life for many years.

Eventually leaving Canada and moving to England, liberty became a British citizen, intending to spend the rest of her life in a quirky, 500-year-old cottage in rural Northamptonshire. But the universe had other plans for her, and after several years, due to circumstances very much beyond her control, she was forced to return to Calgary to begin a new life.

As a single mum in the 1980s, liberty returned to school and studied social work, later receiving certification as a hypnotist to further help her counselling clients. In the '90s, she studied with the well-respected School of Homeopathy (Devon, England), where she received top marks while earning her Practitioner's Diploma.

One of the highlights of liberty's life was signing a contract with a top literary agency in London, through which she has had some syndication work in various countries, including a weekly column in the Dubai version of "Hello!" magazine. Currently, the agency is seeking a publisher for liberty's fascinating manuscript, "The Power and Simplicity of Self-Healing", which is currently available both in print and as an ebook.

She has been fortunate in that some of her hobbies, interests and natural abilities have also become her work, such as writing, art, music and being a psychic medium, to name just a few. As a woman who loves to learn, grow and change, there is always something new on liberty's horizon.

CONNECT WITH THE AUTHOR

http://www.libertyforrest.com

http://facebook.com/libertyspage

http://twitter.com/libertyforrest

OTHER BOOKS BY LIBERTY FORREST

At the time of this writing, liberty has published, and will be publishing, several other books in both print form and as ebooks, some of which are listed below. Visit www.libertyforrest.com for more information.

"The Power and Simplicity of Self-Healing"

"Incredibly interesting and informative! So fantastic, I didn't want it to end. A truly life-changing book."

-- Katie McAlindon, Kettering, England

"Wow! What an amazing book!! Definitely a must-read. It's completely life-changing, helped me to alter my whole way of thinking. I feel like a newer, happier and more positive person. Just what I needed. Perfect!"

-- Ashleigh Marshall, Northampton, England

"Incredible as it seems, using substantial scientific evidence, this book proves that we do have the POWER to heal ourselves, IF we have the knowledge. This book provides us with that knowledge in everyday, down-to-earth, layman's language. Everyone should read this book."

-- A.M. Kandiuk, Toronto, Canada

About *The Power and Simplicity of Self-Healing*:

We've all heard those occasional stories of people who have recovered from untreatable or incurable conditions. There are those who were told they would never walk again - but through sheer determination, they did it. There are those who were riddled with malignant tumours and given a death sentence, but repeatedly visualised perfect healing and they became well.

There are numerous documented reports like these and usually, we think they are flukes, coincidence, or perhaps "miracles". They are so rare and so powerful, the notion that this could be commonplace does not occur to us.

But it should.

The "default setting" for any living organism is survival, yet it is only possible if the organism is inherently able to heal. We think nothing of our ability to recover from illnesses, injuries, broken bones. But why stop there? Why is it impossible to believe that we can heal ourselves of anything more serious than a broken arm or a really bad flu?

It is only because we have not known we could do it. For thousands of years, we have turned to medicine men, healers of all kinds throughout the ages, unaware that each of us possesses the power to create - and to heal - our illnesses.

The Power and Simplicity of Self-Healing is chock full of fascinating information that revolutionises the way we look at illness and healing. This life-changing book encompasses a wide range of seemingly disconnected and unrelated subjects, yet each one is a separate piece of an incredible and complex puzzle. One at a time, liberty explains each of them, ultimately revealing a startlingly simple picture that provides indisputable scientific proof that all of us have the ability to heal ourselves of virtually any illness.

For most of her life, liberty suffered with ill health, some of it life-threatening, much of it just plain miserable and debilitating. For a number of years, she had found great help with homeopathy, believing it to be the be-all and end-all in healing. Although it is extremely powerful and produces miraculous cures, she reached a point where it was no longer helping, nor was anything else. She had run out of hope and any reasonable options.

Her desperate and futile search for wellness took her down many paths from the conventional to the near insane. When it seemed all avenues had been exhausted, in an explosive moment of anger and frustration, she vowed to find a way to heal herself, believing that if other people have done it, then she could do it, too.

With occasional interjections about her own story of suffering and healing, this book covers a multitude of topics in a step-by-step systematic fashion, layering one piece of information on another and building a strong foundation so that all of the pieces are well-connected and logical.

Drawing on a wealth of information from numerous medical professionals, researchers and scientists, along with the metaphysical, mysterious and inexplicable, liberty drops one fascinating piece of the puzzle after another into its rightful place, creating multi-faceted and undeniable proof that self-healing is not only possible and powerful, but very simple for anyone to do. If she can do it - as ill as she was - you can do it, too.

"Soul Food: 101 Inspirational Messages to Nourish and Heal Your Spirit" - short article-length pieces to inspire, encourage, entertain, teach and heal, with such topics as forgiveness, dealing with grief, finding hope, staying positive, finding your strength, letting go of the past, getting through trauma, or dealing with difficult relationships.

"Insightful, intuitive, instinctive, introspective - and always interesting!"

-- Tony Smith (Northamptonshire Evening Telegraph)

"Reading liberty's inspirational writing is like having my own personal rainbow delivered to me every time "

-- Debra Carney, Florida, USA

"The Gift"

"A very inspirational book. The characters pull you right into the story and keep you reading. I laughed, cried, and was in awe. Truly a wonderful writer!"

-- Melinda L. Clarkson, Oregon, USA

"A wonderful, endearing book, with all the ingredients to stir your imagination and lift your hearts. The story tells a tale of how each member of a family deals with a difficult emotional situation. It will wring your heart out like a sponge, and yet it is beautifully orchestrated, showing raw emotions and how the family members deal with their own demons. I was so deeply moved by this book, I have ordered a copy for every member of the family and all of my friends!

"With an exceptionally emotionally charged ending, I cannot say enough about this book. It leaves you wanting more, wishing it didn't end, wishing you could know more about what happens to this family. (The author) is so descriptive and lets us known the characters so intimately, that we cannot help but feel that they are real people and we really want to follow their lives after the story ends...

"If you never buy another book again, you must buy this one! It is so powerful, so moving, so beautifully written, it is guaranteed to be an extremely satisfying read!"

-- Mrs. Charles Senior, Bolton, England

About *The Gift*: This is a heartbreaking, emotionally charged novel. It is the story of a family's journey through a very difficult and turbulent year. Already having endured many hardships, this family is fractured without even realising it until the youngest child becomes critically ill.

With Christmas approaching, the little girl's health takes a dramatic turn for the worse. Her parents and brothers quietly begin falling apart and it doesn't take long before the fractures are enormous cracks, threatening to shatter the family completely.

The Spirit Within

Four-year-old Angelina watches as her family is forced to confront its demons, and she longs for her parents and brother to find their way to healing. But as with many healing journeys, things must get a lot worse before even beginning to get better.

This story is certain to move its readers to tears as they connect and identify with each member of the Lane family. Meet Angelina and the others: Wife and mother, Kathy, so lost in her own emotions that she withdraws from life, entirely in denial; her husband, Robert, guilt-ridden and feeling inadequate; teen son, James, consumed by his own anger to the point of self-destruction; and Elijah, a wise old soul at the age of ten, trying desperately to be the glue that holds his family together. Follow these troubled hearts, who are lost and struggling to find their way through the darkness and who have lost all hope of ever finding the light.

"Unmotherly Love" (expected release in early 2013) - a powerful autobiographical book about liberty's complicated relationship with her mother, who was the greatest source of pain and damage in liberty's turbulent life, and because of this, was ultimately her greatest teacher.

"Unmotherly Love" unravels some of the emotional and psychological issues that many women face in their relationships with their mothers, and with their daughters. Often these are the most powerful relationships women have, shaping their lives until they figure out how to shape them for themselves. Understanding their mothers helps women to understand themselves. Making sense of the paths they walked with their mothers, and appreciating that the twists and turns were ultimately for their benefit, this book will help women find great strength, peace and healing, thereby

improving their relationships with their mothers, and with their daughters as well.

The Spirit Within

Made in the USA
Charleston, SC
02 November 2014